CONTRIBUTORS AND CONSULTANTS

THE GOLDEN BOOK ENCYCLOPEDIA

VOLUME VII—GHOSTS TO HOUSE PLANTS

In Sixteen Accurate, Fact-filled Volumes Dramatically Illustrated with More Than 6,000 Color Pictures

THE ONLY ENCYCLOPEDIA FOR YOUNG GRADE-SCHOOL CHILDREN

ACCURATE AND AUTHORITATIVE

ENTERTAININGLY WRITTEN AND ILLUSTRATED TO
MAKE LEARNING AN ADVENTURE

by Bertha Morris Parker

*Formerly of the Laboratory Schools, University of Chicago
Research Associate, Chicago Natural History Museum*

GOLDEN PRESS · NEW YORK

THIRD PRINTING, 1960

© Copyright 1959 by Golden Press, Inc. Designed and produced by Artists and
Writers Press, Inc. Printed in the U.S.A. by Western Printing and Lithographing
Company. Published by Golden Press, Inc., Rockefeller Center, New York 20, N. Y.

Illustrations from GOLDEN BOOKS, published by Golden Press, Inc., New York, © 1946, 1949,
1950, 1951, 1952, 1953, 1954, 1955, 1956, 1957 by Golden Press, Inc.; and from the Basic
Science Education Series (Unitext), published by Row, Peterson and Company, Evanston, Illinois,
© 1941, 1942, 1943, 1945, 1946, 1947, 1949, 1952, 1957, 1958, 1959 by Row, Peterson and Company.

Famous Ghosts of Stories and Legends

GHOSTS No one ever really saw or heard a ghost. There are no true haunted houses. But many people think that they have seen or heard ghosts. And many people have moved away from houses because they thought that they were haunted.

This is the true story of one "haunted" house. No one lived in this house. Many people who drove past it at night reported that they saw a ghost run through the house from front to back with a lighted lamp. They did not actually see the ghost itself, but they could see the flickering light of its lamp shining out of first one window and then another.

Someone finally tracked down this ghost. It turned out that the old house had wavy glass in its windows. When the light from a car struck first one window and then another, the wavy glass reflected the light in a peculiar way. Backing a car past the house made the ghost seem to run from the back of the house to the front.

Ghosts are supposed to be the spirits of dead people. They are supposed to look much as they looked when they were alive except that often they have no heads. They are supposed to be able to go through locked doors or closed windows and to talk, but with queer "spooky" voices.

There are some famous ghosts that are "seen" rather often. Many old castles in England and Ireland are "haunted." Of course, if anyone is told that a ghost will appear, he easily imagines that he sees it, especially at night in pale moonlight.

One of England's most famous ghosts is the giant red-haired ghost of Glamis Castle. Another is the ghost of Dick Turpin, a famous English highwayman. People say that it gallops down a steep hill three times a year. The ghost of Sir Francis Drake has been seen many times riding in a black coach drawn by headless horses.

England's most haunted house is a rectory in Essex. Among its ghosts are two headless horsemen, a nun, and a lady who cries, "Don't, Carlos, don't!"

Shakespeare put ghosts in some of his plays. Other writers have put ghosts in their plays and stories, too. Ghosts are fun to read about even though we know there are no real ones. (See SUPERSTITIONS.)

GIANT PANDA Twenty-five years ago almost no one had ever seen a giant panda. And not many more people had ever heard of one. This animal lives in a small region in the mountains of western China. Scientists first knew about the giant panda when a missionary sent the skin and some bones of one to a museum in Paris.

For years after that, explorers tried to capture a panda. But no one succeeded until 1937. Then one was caught and sent to the Brookfield Zoo in Chicago. Since then several others have been caught.

When the first panda reached the zoo, the keepers wondered what to feed it. In its home the panda eats nothing but bamboo. But in the zoo it ate other things. Cornmeal mush was one of them.

A panda looks like a big stuffed toy. It is a clown and goes through many queer antics. In a zoo there is always a crowd around the panda cage.

Many people think that the panda is a kind of bear. But it is really much more closely related to raccoons than to bears.

GIANTS Many of our favorite stories have giants in them. There are, for instance, many giants in Greek myths. Atlas held the world on his shoulders. Prometheus brought fire to the earth. Both Atlas and Prometheus were Titans, all of whom were giants. Cyclops was a one-eyed giant in Greek myths. In Norse myths the frost giants waged an unending war with both gods and men.

The Bible tells the story of how the boy David killed Goliath with a slingshot. Goliath was a giant.

In *Gulliver's Travels* Gulliver visited a whole country of giants—the Brobdingnagians. The giant in the story of Jack and the beanstalk is perhaps the best-known of storybook giants.

Every country has tales of its own giants. Among the legends of the United States, for instance, are many about Paul Bunyan, a giant, and his amazing feats.

Circus Giant

Fairy Tale Giant

Cyclops

Circus Midget

Paul Bunyan

There are no giants in real life as big as storybook giants. Many men and women are several inches or even a foot or two taller than the average person. Many of the boys on basketball teams are so tall that in a way they are giants. But these tall people do not have the great weight and strength of the giants of storybooks.

Scientists know now that a tiny gland in the head has a great deal to do with a person's size. This gland is the pituitary gland. If a person is much taller than his fellows, he can, as a rule, give his pituitary gland the credit—or the blame.

In many stories of giants, the giants are bad-tempered and cruel. Actually a person's size does not have anything to do with his disposition.

It may be that our earliest ancestors were giants. At least, scientists have found bones of some early men who seem to have been giants. We may have come by our ideas of giants quite naturally. (See BIBLE STORIES; BODY, HUMAN; DWARFS; MYTHS AND LEGENDS.)

GIBRALTAR Both a strait and a "rock" have the name of "Gibraltar." The Strait of Gibraltar is the gateway from the Atlantic Ocean into the Mediterranean Sea and separates Europe from Africa. The Rock of Gibraltar is a high, rocky point of land that reaches out into the strait from the peninsula of Spain.

In ancient times the Rock of Gibraltar was called one of the two Pillars of Hercules. The second "pillar" was across the strait on the African shore.

The Strait of Gibraltar is about nine miles wide at its narrowest point. At its widest point it measures about 24 miles. It is a part of one of the most traveled seaways in the world. Ships go through this strait on their way from western Europe and the Americas to southern Europe, northern Africa, and western Asia. The building of the Suez Canal to join the Mediterranean with the Red Sea made the Strait

Rock of Gibraltar

of Gibraltar also a part of the shortest water route from western Europe and eastern North America to the Far East.

The Spaniards and the Moors fought for the Rock of Gibraltar for several centuries. But in 1704 the British and Dutch seized it. A few years later, in 1713, Britain was given full possession of it by the terms of the Treaty of Utrecht. The Rock of Gibraltar still belongs to Britain.

The Rock is only about two and three-quarters miles long and three-quarters of a mile wide. But during a war the country that owns it can keep the ships of an enemy from passing through the strait. Britain has made the Rock into a great fortress. There is a harbor for warships at the base. The Rock is so well protected that "as safe as the Rock of Gibraltar" is a common saying. Gibraltar is one of the world's "great little places." (See BRITISH EMPIRE.)

GILBERT AND SULLIVAN *The Mikado, The Pirates of Penzance,* and *H.M.S. Pinafore* are gay operettas written more than 60 years ago by two Englishmen— William S. Gilbert and Arthur Sullivan. Gilbert and Sullivan wrote a dozen or so operettas together. Gilbert wrote the words for all of them. Sullivan wrote the music. Among their other operettas are *The Gondoliers, Iolanthe, Trial by Jury,* and *The Yeomen of the Guard.*

H.M.S. Pinafore, one of their early operettas, is one of the gayest. All the action in it takes place on shipboard. "H.M.S." stands for "Her Majesty's Ship." Three of the songs in the operetta are "I'm Called Little Buttercup," "I Am the Captain of the Pinafore," and "When I Was a Lad." *Pinafore* was such a success that at one time 90 different companies were singing it. All the Gilbert and Sullivan operettas were so well liked that a new theater—the Savoy— was built just for them.

In these operettas there are songs called patter songs. They are not easy to sing. The words must be sung very fast but very clearly. If they are not understood, much of the fun of the operetta is lost.

There is so much gaiety in their operettas that it is hard to believe that Gilbert and Sullivan did not enjoy working together. But they did not. They were always quarreling. At last they became so angry with each other that they decided that they could never work together again.

They wrote their last operetta in 1896. But their operettas are still popular. In the United States there are about 5,000 performances every year. In other countries there are many, too. (See OPERETTAS.)

The Mikado

The Pirates of Penzance

H.M.S. Pinafore

Patience

WILLIAM S. GILBERT

ARTHUR SULLIVAN

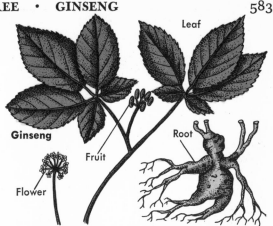

Ginseng

Leaf

Fruit

Flower

Root

GINGERBREAD TREE The doom palm grows in Egypt and some of the lands near by. Another name for it is "gingerbread tree." This palm has a red fruit about the size of an apple. Inside the fruit there is a single seed. The pulpy part of the fruit around the seed is good to eat. It tastes a little like gingerbread.

The fruit of the gingerbread tree has been eaten for thousands of years. It has been found in Egyptian tombs 5,000 years old. The ancient Egyptians made a practice of burying food with people when they died.

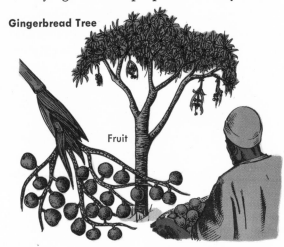

Gingerbread Tree

Fruit

GINKGO In America the ginkgo is often called the maidenhair tree. Its leaves are fan-shaped. Although the ginkgo is a distant relative of the pines and firs, it is not an evergreen. Its leaves turn yellow and fall off in the autumn.

The fruit of the ginkgo has an unpleasant smell. But the seed inside is good to eat.

This tree has lived on the earth for a very long time. The ginkgo trees we have now are almost exactly like their ancestors of ten million years ago.

Once the ginkgo had many close relatives. But they all disappeared. The ginkgo, too, would probably have disappeared if the Chinese and Japanese had not planted ginkgo trees in their temple gardens. They thought of these trees as sacred.

Ginkgoes are found in many cities. They are well liked partly because they have few insect enemies. (See PLANT KINGDOM.)

GINSENG The plant we call ginseng grows wild in China and in the eastern part of the United States. It is also cultivated in the United States, China, and Japan.

Ginseng has pretty red berries in the fall, but the plant is not raised for them. It is raised for its roots. They bring high prices in China. So far as anyone knows, the roots are of little real use. But for hundreds of years the Chinese have thought that the roots would cure many kinds of sickness. There are Chinese stories which tell how wild animals protect this wonderful plant. There are other Chinese stories which tell that the plant travels underground to escape its enemies.

Probably the shape of the ginseng roots gave the Chinese the idea that they would be good medicine. "Ginseng" means "likeness of men." Wild roots bring higher prices than cultivated ones because they are more likely to be shaped like men. Cultivated roots look very much like parsnips.

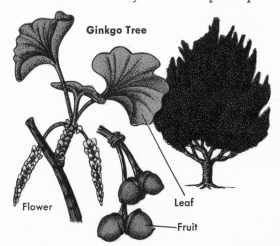

Ginkgo Tree

Flower

Leaf

Fruit

Giotto Painting "The Life of Christ"

GIOTTO (1276-1337) In Italy, not far from Florence, a barefoot boy tended sheep and drew pictures in the sand with his toes. Now and then with a sharp pebble he would scratch a picture on a flat rock. Purple mountains rose up in the distance. It was very quiet in the fields except for the tinkling bells on the sheep.

One day while Giotto was drawing a picture of one of his sheep, a man came riding by. A glance at the picture told the rider that the boy was gifted. He jumped off his horse and shouted, "You must come to Florence and help me in my bottega." A bottega was a workshop. The man was the greatest Italian artist of the time, Cimabue.

Giotto was only ten years old then, but his parents let him go to Florence. He was called an apprentice. Cimabue had several other apprentices. His apprentices all lived with him. They worked hard in the workshop during the daytime. But they had fun together in the evenings.

Giotto liked Florence. The little red carts drawn by donkeys made pleasant rattling noises on the stony streets. There were many wonderful statues, paintings, and buildings to see. The rich people of the city wore beautiful velvet clothes.

Day after day Giotto washed brushes, ground colors, and practiced painting. At that time oil painting had not been invented. Cimabue and many other painters of the time were fresco painters. Fresco is water-color painting done on wet plaster.

When Giotto was still a boy, Cimabue said to him, "You are now a greater artist than I." He let Giotto draw the sheep whenever he needed sheep in his pictures. Giotto could draw sheep better than anyone else in Florence because he had studied them so much as a child.

When Giotto was a young man he set up a workshop of his own. Before long he was called to Rome to make a mosaic showing Jesus walking on the Sea of Galilee. A mosaic is a picture made of many tiny pieces of glass or stone. In Rome Giotto learned much about lifelike painting that helped him to be a great artist.

Giotto became an architect as well as a painter. His greatest work as an architect is the famous bell tower of the cathedral at Florence. This bell tower is usually called Giotto's Tower.

Giotto's greatest paintings are the frescoes in a small church in Padua. There are 38 frescoes in the one little church. It took Giotto six years to paint them.

The frescoes in Padua tell the story of the Mother of Jesus and of Jesus Himself. Giotto has been called the greatest storytelling artist. The people in his pictures look almost as if they were cut out of stone, they are so rounded. Each picture is much like a stage on which people are acting.

With their hands they show joy, pain, longing, and deep sorrow.

In the Padua frescoes there are soft colors of rose, pale blue, and gray-green. Frescoes are always light because the color soaks into the plaster.

Giotto was so great a painter that every art student studies his pictures. One famous writer about art says, "I see no greater artist in history." (See MOSAIC; PAINTERS AND PAINTING; RENAISSANCE.)

GIRAFFE The giraffe is the tallest of all animals. A full-grown giraffe is about three times as tall as a man. Its front legs are so long that they look like stilts. Its neck is very long, too.

Giraffes are found wild only in Africa. They live in hot, dry regions. Fortunately, they can go for weeks at a time without drinking any water. They get some water from their food.

Usually a giraffe eats tree leaves. But by spreading its front legs far apart it can stoop down to eat grass.

Lions are the giraffe's worst enemies. Giraffes can kick with great force. They can protect themselves from many of their enemies in this way. But if they could not run very fast, and if their spots did not make them hard to see when they are in among trees, all the giraffes might have been eaten by lions long ago. (See HOOFED ANIMALS; PROTECTIVE COLORING.)

The giraffe's long neck has only as many vertebrae as that of a mouse. Though they both have seven bones, those in the giraffe's neck are much larger. Both the length of its neck and its 18-inch tongue make it possible for the giraffe to reach the leaves on trees which make up the large part of a giraffe's diet.

Giraffes spread their legs to stoop down.

GLACIERS A glacier is a river or great moving sheet of ice. Rivers of ice are always in valleys. They are often called valley glaciers. Great moving sheets of ice are often called icecaps.

A glacier begins as a snowfield. Little by little the snow becomes solid ice. The ice grows thicker and begins to move. The snowfield has become a glacier.

A valley, glacier moves down its valley. It may move less than a foot a day. It may move more than a hundred. All valley glaciers move, but some of them do not seem to be doing so. A glacier looks as if it were standing still if the ice at the end melts as fast as more ice is pushed down. An icecap moves outward in all directions. But it may move quite a bit faster at some places than at others.

As glaciers move, great cracks appear in them. These cracks are called crevasses. Crevasses make the exploring of glaciers exciting and dangerous.

Glaciers scratch the rocks they move over. They grind up rocks, too. As a rule a glacier pushes along great piles of rock rubbish. These piles are called moraines.

Valley glaciers are common in the Alps and Himalayas. They are common, too, in Norway, Alaska, and western Canada. Glacier National Park, which has several glaciers, is in northwestern United States. Antarctica and Greenland are almost completely covered with big sheets of ice.

The climate of the world has changed many times. Suppose it should get so warm that all the glaciers melted. Then the water in the oceans would rise 100 feet. A great deal of what is now dry land would then be under the sea. (See ALPS; FIORD; HIMALAYAS; ICE AGE.)

Rock Scratched by a Glacier

A Retreating Glacier

Blowing a Glass Flask

Cutting off the Blown Flask

GLASS Imagining that a substance suddenly disappears helps us see how important it is. Suppose glass should suddenly disappear. The windows in our buildings would be just openings. There would be no windshields or window glass in our cars. Walls made of glass bricks would be gone. People would have no eyeglasses or opera glasses or binoculars. Microscopes, telescopes, and cameras would be useless without their glass lenses and mirrors.

Scientists would have no glassware to use in experiments. Doctors would have no fever thermometers. There would be no glass tumblers or plates or cups and saucers. No greenhouses or show windows or showcases! No electric lamp bulbs or radio and television tubes! No bottles on our medicine shelves! No glass threads to weave into cloth! No glass wool in walls to shut heat in or out! No pretty vases or other glass ornaments! The world would be different indeed without glass.

The very first glass was made by nature in volcanoes. It is called volcanic glass, or obsidian. Ancient man fashioned it into spearheads and arrow tips.

Just when people learned to make glass no one knows. A story nearly 2,000 years old tells that some Phoenician sailors were cooking their meal one day on a sandy shore. To hold their kettle up above the fire they used two chunks of the material with which their boat was loaded. This material was natron, or soda ash. After the fire was out, the sailors found that some of the sand that had been heated under the fire had been made into glass.

Probably this story is not true. But it may help us remember that glass is made mostly of sand and that soda ash or some similar chemical must be mixed with the sand to make it melt when it is heated.

Making glass is a little like making candy. The sand is the sugar. The chemical that makes the sand melt takes the place of water that dissolves the sugar. Different materials are added to make different kinds of glass, just as flavorings are added to make different kinds of candy. The mixture is cooked until it is done. Then it is made into any shape wanted.

There is one big difference between making glass and making candy. For glass the mixture must be heated extremely hot in big furnaces. It must be heated in clay pots; iron ones would not stand the heat.

There are many, many recipes for candy. Perhaps there are even more for glass. At least there are over 20,000.

Making glass sounds simpler than it is. One trick in making good glass is to start with very pure materials. Even tiny bits of some impurity may spoil a batch of glass. A trace of iron oxide, for instance, will give glass an ugly greenish color. Another trick in glassmaking is to cool the finished glass properly. A whole year was needed to cool the glass for the mirror of the giant Palomar telescope.

There has been some man-made glass for several thousand years. The Egyptians made glass beads and put thin layers of glass, or glaze, over clay figures. The Romans learned how to lift a lump of soft glass on a hollow iron rod and blow it into such shapes as vases and bottles.

During the Middle Ages Venice was the leading glassmaking city of the world.

Venetian glassmakers blew fairylike goblets, vases, and other wares. They knew how to put wonderful colors in their glass.

There were beautiful glass vases before there was any window glass. It was not at all easy to take a bubble of glass and flatten it out into a flat sheet. But ways were found of doing so. Glass windows were then possible—not at first for homes, because of the cost, but for churches. In the Middle Ages stained glass windows were made of small pieces of beautifully colored glass held together by strips of lead.

For centuries all glassware was scarce and expensive. For every piece of glass had to be made by hand. It took a long time to make a good piece of glass and a very long time to train a good glass blower.

But at last machines came into the picture. In 1827 an American, Enoch Robinson, invented a way of pressing glass into shape in a mold instead of blowing it. Another American, Michael J. Owens, invented a bottlemaking machine in 1899. Machines were invented for making sheets of glass so clear and smooth that they are almost invisible. Scientists still blow glass into specially shaped pieces of apparatus that they need. But for the most part only the most beautiful and expensive glass is now made by hand.

Glass is fireproof. It is waterproof. Most acids cannot eat into it. Rats, mice, and insects cannot destroy it. It can be very beautiful. But it breaks!

Glassmakers have made great strides in overcoming this big objection to glass. They have added boron to glass to keep it from breaking easily when it is heated. Such glass can be used for oven baking dishes. They have made shatterproof glass for cars by sandwiching a piece of plastic in between two layers of glass. They have made glass for show windows that, if it breaks, will break into such tiny powdery pieces that no passer-by will be hurt. They have even been able to make very expensive glass that is almost unbreakable. With glass needed for so many things, we can be sure that many people are at work trying to make it better and better. (See LENSES; MICROSCOPE; MIRRORS; SAND; STAINED GLASS; TELESCOPE.)

GOATS Male goats have beards. In other ways goats look a great deal like sheep. But they are not such well-behaved animals. They are hard to keep in a field.

Many goats are raised in mountain lands where the ground is rocky and the pasture is poor. They will even thrive in cities with nothing to eat but waste vegetables and a few scrubby bushes. Goats seem to like to go exploring. They explore gardens, piles of garbage, and rubbish heaps. But they do not, as some people think, eat tin cans.

Wild Goat

Saanen

Angora

In many countries goat's milk and cheese are very important foods. The goats may be driven from door to door and milked for each customer. Goats are also raised for their hair. They furnish mohair.

There are many kinds of goats. The picture shows two of the kinds people raise. The long-haired Angora is raised for its hair. The Saanen is a good milk goat. The Toggenburg and the Nubian are other good milk goats. A wild goat, the markhor, is sometimes called the king of goats. It is more than three feet high, and its horns are over five feet long. It lives in the high Himalayas. The American Rocky Mountain goat is not really a goat. It is an antelope instead. (See CHEESE; DOMESTICATED ANIMALS; HOOFED ANIMALS; MILK.)

GOATSUCKERS The whip-poor-will belongs to a bird family with the odd name of goatsuckers. The chuck-will's-widow, the poor-will, and the nighthawk are other goatsuckers found in the United States. The family got its name because people long ago thought that the nightjar was able to milk goats. The nightjar is a goatsucker common in Europe, where many goats are raised for milk. Of course, neither the nightjar nor any other bird in the family can milk goats. It is hard to see how the idea got started.

It is much easier to see how the different birds in the family got their names.

The whip-poor-will, poor-will, and chuck-will's-widow got their names from their calls. In many places the call of one or another of these birds is a common sound at night. A single whip-poor-will may utter its call hundreds of times without stopping. The nighthawk flies about at dusk and looks somewhat like a hawk. The "jar" in the nightjar's name means "harsh sound." Like all the other goatsuckers, the nightjar is a night bird.

Many people have seen nighthawks but have never seen any of the other goatsuckers. The other birds in the family are much more shy than nighthawks. Nighthawks often nest in cities and are seen swooping about over city buildings. The other goatsuckers are country birds.

Goatsuckers do not build nests. They usually lay their eggs on the bare ground or on beds of leaves. Nighthawks often lay their eggs on roofs that are covered with gravel. All the goatsuckers have coloring that makes it hard to see them when they are sitting on their eggs.

These birds have wide mouths and short bills. Some of them have whiskers. Their big mouths are well fitted for catching insects in the air. The birds simply open their mouths and fly fast. Their mouths are like tiny butterfly nets. All the goatsuckers are friends of ours because they catch great numbers of harmful insects. (See BIRDS; PROTECTIVE COLORING.)

Whip-poor-will

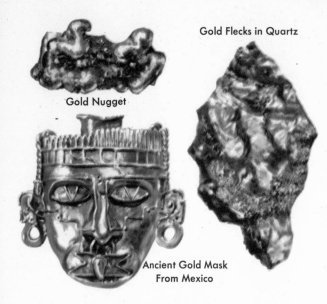

Gold Nugget

Gold Flecks in Quartz

Ancient Gold Mask
From Mexico

GOLD Wars have been fought for gold. Explorers have braved many dangers to find it. The discovery of gold has brought a rush of settlers to many places. In the Middle Ages alchemists spent their lives trying to change cheaper metals into gold.

Gold has been known since the beginning of history. Surprisingly, it was known long before the common metal aluminum. Aluminum was hard to discover because it is always joined with other materials. Gold often is found free.

Gold was used for ornaments long before it was used as money. It was much wanted for its beauty. Ancient gold ornaments have been found in many places.

As money, gold served well. It was scarce, but not too scarce. It was lasting. And it could easily be shaped into coins. Much money today is paper money, but governments still have stores of gold.

Since gold does not spoil, it can be reworked again and again. The gold in a ring bought today may once have been part of an Inca ornament. It may have been a coin in a pirate's buried treasure. Of course, it may have been mined only a few months ago in a modern gold mine.

The first gold was found on or near the surface of the ground. The earliest way of mining it was to dig up gravel that had gold in it and wash away everything except the gold. Gold can be mined in this way because it is very heavy. Chunks of gold are called nuggets. Most of them are tiny, but some are quite large. The "Welcome Stranger" nugget found in Australia was so big that it sold for $52,500.

Today most gold is mined deep underground. The gold is found in veins in the solid rock. Some mines are a mile deep.

Gold in jewelry and ornaments is usually mixed with other metals to make it harder. The finest gold jewelry is marked 18K (18 carat). It has 18 parts of gold to 6 parts of another metal. In 14K gold there are 14 parts of gold to 10 parts of another metal. Pure gold would be 24K.

Long ago people discovered that gold can be hammered into very thin sheets, or gold leaf. Some gold leaf is so thin that 350,000 sheets make a pile only an inch high. Gold leaf is used to make letters on books and signs and to decorate china, furniture, and even buildings.

Not all gold goes into money and decorations. Much gold, for instance, goes into fillings for teeth.

Although gold mining began thousands of years ago, all the gold that has ever been mined could be stored easily on the first floor of the White House in Washington, D.C. The amount added each year to the world's supply could be put in a box 5 feet by 5 feet by 6 feet.

Today South Africa leads all countries in the amount of gold mined. Canada, the Soviet Union, and the United States run a race for second. (See ALCHEMY; DENTISTRY; ELEMENTS; JEWELRY; METALS; MIDAS; MINES AND MINING; MONEY; YUKON.)

Gold Crystal   Gold Ore

The Longest Suspension Bridge in the World

GOLDEN GATE A short and narrow strip of sea leads from the Pacific Ocean into San Francisco Bay. This strip of sea is called the Golden Gate. Another name for such a strip of water is "strait." The Golden Gate, then, is a strait.

The famous explorer Sir Francis Drake sighted this strait on his trip around the world in the late 1500's. Some people think Drake gave the strait its name. But John C. Frémont, an American explorer, claimed that he named the Golden Gate.

The name had real meaning during the Gold Rush to California in 1849. Many people sailed through it on their way to hunt for gold. Everyone who has seen the waters of the Golden Gate glitter in the sunset agrees that the name is still a good one.

San Francisco is on one side of the Golden Gate. One of the world's greatest bridges, the Golden Gate Bridge, stretches more than a mile from San Francisco across the strait. (See BRIDGES; CALIFORNIA; SAN FRANCISCO; STRAITS.)

GOLDENROD In many parts of America goldenrod in bloom along the roadsides means that fall is on its way. Goldenrod gets its name from the bright yellow color of its flowers.

Goldenrod belongs to the composite family, the biggest of all the families of flowering plants. Like all other plants in this big family, its flowers are made up of a number of tiny flowerets.

There are many different kinds of goldenrod—nearly 100 in all. Some kinds have rough stems, some have smooth stems, and some have stems covered with hair. The leaves of the goldenrods differ, too. Some are narrow, some wide. Some have toothed edges while others have smooth edges.

Goldenrod grows in many places. One kind, called seaside goldenrod, grows in salt marshes by the sea. Alpine goldenrod grows on mountaintops. The large-leafed goldenrod grows in damp woods.

Unfortunately, many people believe that goldenrod gives them hayfever. Usually, however, goldenrod is not to blame. Hayfever is more often caused by pollen from ragweed, which blooms at the same time as goldenrod. (See FLOWER FAMILIES.)

GOLDENRODS

Comet

Black Moor

Calico
Fringetail

FANCY GOLDFISH

GOLDFISH All the fish in the two pictures are goldfish, although they do not look very much alike. All these kinds, and many more, too, have come from the wild goldfish that have lived for centuries in the streams of China and Japan.

The wild goldfish is not a very pretty fish. It is usually dull green, and it has small fins and a short tail.

The Chinese found out long ago that it is easy to keep goldfish in small ponds and aquariums. The idea of getting more beautiful fish came when the Chinese noticed that some of the dull-green fish had spots of gold. They watched carefully for fish with spots of gold. They took good care of these fish and their eggs. Some of the fish that came from the eggs had more gold spots than their parents.

The Chinese kept on choosing and saving the fish that were best. Finally they had fish that were all gold.

At least 400 years ago the Japanese began raising goldfish. Both the Chinese and the Japanese set about getting goldfish of new colors. In time they had black, silver, and spotted, or calico, goldfish.

The Chinese and Japanese found, too, that color was not the only thing that could be changed. By careful choosing and mating they were able to get fish with flowing tails, very thin scales, and bulging eyes.

Oranda

Fringetail

Now goldfish are raised in many parts of the world. Millions are sold each year for ponds and aquariums. And goldfish breeders are still working to get new kinds.

Like any other pet, a goldfish must have proper care and the right kind of place to live. A two-inch fish needs at least two gallons of water. The water must have oxygen in it or the fish cannot breathe. Some oxygen gets into the water of an aquarium from the air that touches the surface.

Plants in an aquarium help furnish oxygen, too. Green plants throw oxygen away when they are making food for themselves. At the same time, they use up the carbon dioxide the fish breathe out. Snails help keep an aquarium clean. With plenty of plants and snails, the water in an aquarium should not have to be changed often.

Food made of such things as dried insects and shrimp can be bought for goldfish. Goldfish should not be overfed. They should never be given more food at one time than they can eat up in about five minutes. And they should not be fed more than once a day. (See AQUARIUM; PETS.)

GOODYEAR, CHARLES (1800-1860) Millions of people around the world today ride about on rubber tires. They all owe a debt to Charles Goodyear.

Rubber was known long before the time of Goodyear, but it had serious drawbacks. In cold weather it would become hard and crack. In warm weather it would get sticky and give off a bad odor.

Many people tried to find some way to make rubber into a more satisfactory material. Charles Goodyear was one of them. He carried on hundreds of experiments. He mixed many other substances with rubber to see what effect they would have.

One day in 1839, while he was working on one of his experiments, he accidentally dropped a piece of rubber on a hot stove. This rubber had been mixed with sulfur. The rubber and sulfur charred but they did not burn. When Goodyear tried out this rubber, he found that it was better than any other rubber he had seen. It did not get sticky and give off a bad odor when it was warmed. Cold did not make it crack. The sulfur and the heat together had changed the rubber in some way.

Goodyear's way of preparing rubber is called "vulcanization." The word came from "Vulcan," the Roman god of fire.

Goodyear was born in New Haven, Conn. His father was an inventor of farm machinery. Goodyear did not make a fortune from his discovery about rubber. In fact, at one point in his life he was put into debtor's prison. He was still deeply in debt when he died. Of course, Goodyear had no way of guessing that gasoline automobiles would be invented and that rubber would be used in tires by the billions of pounds. (See INVENTIONS; RUBBER.)

Goodyear's accident led to a great discovery.

An
Egyptian
Lawgiver

GOVERNMENT We all live under some kind of government. It may be a government in which the people choose their own rulers. On the other hand, the top ruler may be a king or a queen who inherited the right to rule. The ruler may be a dictator who seized the powers of a ruler. In some of the out-of-the-way corners of the earth the rulers are tribal chieftains.

A government may be good or it may be bad. Some people believe that all government is bad. They think that there should be no government. These people are called anarchists. But there are not many anarchists. Government came about because people wanted things they could not get for themselves. Doing without government would mean that everyone would be "on his own." With people crowded together as they are today, no sensible person believes in anarchy.

Government began without any deliberate planning. Our early ancestors did not come together and say, "Now we have to have some kind of government. What kind shall we have?" Instead, it developed gradually as different things were needed.

Even when people had not formed any groups larger than single families there was government of a very simple kind. The fathers and mothers were, in a way, rulers.

But the dangers in early times were so great that, little by little, families banded together. Several families could protect themselves more easily than single families could. The first groups were made up of families related to one another.

One early kind of group is called a patriarchal clan. This kind of group appeared when people became herders instead of hunters. "Patriarch" comes from the word for father. Sons, when they married, did not leave their family group. Their sons, in turn, stayed on. In time a rather big group, or clan, grew up. The father of the whole clan—the patriarch—was looked up to as the wisest member of the group. His word came to be law.

Some of the early bands of people became larger groups, or tribes. Groups often grew by conquering other groups. In the bigger groups some kind of rule was needed even more than in the smaller groups. Disputes between members of a tribe had to be settled, and the tribe had to be led in warfare against other tribes. In tribes a chieftain took the place of the patriarch. Since his most important duty was to protect his people, he was usually a good fighter. In return for his leading them in battle his people were willing to do as he said. When the chieftain of a tribe died, his son might be accepted as ruler.

In the early days of tribes the chieftain was the ruler of a certain group of people. He was not the ruler of a certain part of the earth. Usually the tribes moved about from place to place. But in time the tribes settled in definite regions. Then rulers became lords of the land as well as lords of the people. Nations began.

The story of nations is a long story of experiments with different kinds of government. In the great days of ancient Egypt the ruler was called a "pharaoh." The pharaoh was rich and powerful. His people had little freedom. Their work was planned for them by the government. They had almost no chance to think for themselves.

The pharaoh himself did not do all the work of ruling. He had soldiers, tax collectors, judges, and priests to help him.

The great power of the pharaoh is easily explained. With huge waterworks he controlled the water of the Nile. The very life of the people depended on this water. Besides, the Egyptians thought of him as a god. In spite of his great power over his people, the pharaoh was not really free either. Customs made it impossible for him to do exactly as he pleased.

None of us would like to live under a government like ancient Egypt's. But one of the ideas of the ancient Egyptians and also of other great nations of their time is very important in the story of government. They had the idea of empire—of building many weak groups into one strong group.

Very different from the government of ancient Egypt was that of Athens in the golden age of Greece. Athens, after trying other kinds of government, became a democracy. "Democracy" comes from two Greek words that mean "people" and "rule." The people of Athens ruled themselves.

Although the government of Athens was a democracy, not everyone could have a share in it. Women could not vote. Slaves could not. Neither could men who had not been born in Athens. But every *citizen* could vote. Every citizen could hold office. And every citizen could serve on a jury.

Ancient Rome, like Athens, tried out several kinds of government. At the time of Rome's greatest power it was ruled by an emperor. His chief helpers were the leaders of his armies.

Rome conquered one land after another. Great roads were built to tie the empire together. There was one set of laws for the whole empire. The same weights and measures were used everywhere in the empire. So were the same coins. So was the same language. Some of the Roman emperors were weak. Others were cruel. But the idea of "the same for everyone" was an important idea in government.

The climb from the first simple governments to the governments of today has not been a steady upward climb. In fact, there have been many times of backsliding.

Ten centuries ago in Europe there was almost no government. A person's life was often in danger. Gradually feudalism grew up. This was the time of knights and lords and ladies. The lords lived in castles; they owned much land. Each lord ruled and protected the people on his land. In turn they served him. Feudalism was a step upward from the conditions that went before it

In the past 1,000 years the story of government is the story of many struggles in many places. People have fought for a chance to help rule themselves. They have fought for constitutions—statements of just what their rights are and how the work of the government is to be done. There have

ACTIVITIES
OF
GOVERNMENT

been struggles to separate government and religion. Sometimes people have given up some of their freedom for protection.

Even today the peoples of the world do not all agree as to what kind of government is best. Democracy, communism, and socialism are three different forms of government. But whatever ideas of government they have, people want more from their governments than ever before.

Many people get services from more than one government. They are, we might say, under different layers of government. A person in Chicago, for instance, gets some services from the city and some from Cook County. City and county governments are often called local governments. A Chicagoan gets other services from the state of Illinois and still others from the government of the United States—the federal government. All these governments have the power to pass laws and to see that people obey them. But each government has duties of its own to the people, too. This list names some of the services the different governments provide for a person in any American city:

Local and state governments run schools.

The federal government builds dams.

FEDERAL GOVERNMENT
Maintains army, navy, and air force.
Coins and prints money.
Operates the Weather Bureau.
Operates the Post Office.
Issues patents.
Issues copyrights.
Looks after the rights of Americans in other countries.

STATE GOVERNMENTS
Help provide free schools.
Operate homes for insane and feeble-minded people.
Help take care of the blind.
Administer unemployment insurance for people out of work.
Examine people who want to be doctors, dentists, teachers, and lawyers.
Help supervise banking and insurance.

LOCAL GOVERNMENTS
Provide free libraries.
Pave, light, and clean streets.
Build water supply and sewage systems.
Collect garbage.
Inspect buildings.
Quarantine people with certain contagious diseases.
Keep records of births, deaths, and marriages.

The first duties of a government were to protect its people and to settle disputes among them. These duties are still important. But, as the list shows, there are many newer duties. People ask so much of their governments today that many millions of people in the world are doing government work. (See COMMUNISM; DEMOCRACY; DICTATORS; FASCISM; JUSTICE; LAWS; MONARCHY; SOCIALISM; U. S. CONSTITUTION; U. S. GOVERNMENT.)

Local governments plan parks.

GRAFTING Imagine an apple tree with bright-red Jonathan apples on one limb, Golden Delicious apples on another, and dark-red Winesaps on a third. It is possible to have just such a tree. The process called grafting makes it possible.

Grafting means joining parts of two or more plants together so that they grow to be one plant. The top of a young crab apple tree, for example, may be cut off and the twig of another apple tree put in its place. The inner layer of the bark of a woody plant is called the cambium. It is made up of cells that are alive and growing. In grafting, the two cambium layers must come together.

There are different ways of grafting. The pictures show two of them. The joining is usually protected by a bandage or by a coating of wax.

Fruit trees grown from seeds are not likely to bear fruit just like the fruit that the seeds came from. For the little plant in the seed usually has two different trees as parents. If so, it is sure not to grow into a tree exactly like either parent. The only possible way of getting a new Golden Delicious apple tree is to graft a twig from a Golden Delicious tree on to the stem and roots of some other kind of tree. It may be another apple tree, or a quince tree.

Grafted trees grow faster and bear sooner than trees raised from seed. The stem and roots already have a good start. Another advantage of grafting is that twigs of trees that are easily hurt by disease can be grafted on trees that are hardier.

Fruit trees are not the only plants that are grafted. Grapevines, rosebushes, and lilac bushes are a few of the other plants that are often grafted. But only plants with woody stems can be grafted, and the parts must come from plants that are close relatives. It is fun to think of grafting a rose twig on a walnut tree and getting a rosebush 60 feet tall. But roses and walnuts are not close enough relatives to make such a rosebush possible.

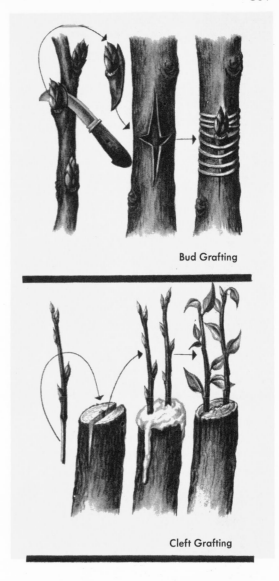

Bud Grafting

Cleft Grafting

Sometimes the top of a grafted plant may be broken off. Then the stem may send out branches and grow into its kind of plant. One man had a funny experience. He grafted twigs of two dwarf catalpa trees to the trunks of two young hardy catalpas. Then he planted the little trees side by side. They grew into very pretty umbrella-shaped trees about ten feet tall. Then a windstorm broke off the top of one tree. Soon the trunk of the damaged tree began to send out branches. It developed into a hardy catalpa nearly 30 feet tall. It and its former twin were a strange pair. (See FRUITS; SEEDS; TREES.)

GRAND CANYON In America there is a great deal of beautiful scenery. The most wonderful sight of all, many people think, is the Grand Canyon. Half a million or so people visit it every year.

This canyon is in northern Arizona. It is a part of the valley of the Colorado River. But what a valley! The canyon is 217 miles long, from 4 to 18 miles wide, and, in places, more than a mile deep. Rising from its floor are mountains higher than the highest mountains in the Appalachians. But their peaks do not reach up as high as the rim of the canyon. In the mountains, as well as in the canyon walls, the layers of rock are beautifully colored.

Trails lead down the steep sides of the canyon to the bottom. The story of a trip to the bottom of the canyon might be called "Climbing Down 500 Million Years." For the rocks at the bottom of the canyon walls are at least 500 million years old.

Most of the layers of rock in the walls of the canyon are sandstone and limestone and shale. These rocks are water-made rocks. They tell that for millions of years this part of the world was under the sea.

At the very bottom of the canyon the rock is granite. Granite is formed from hot liquid rock like the lava that pours out of volcanoes. But it is formed deep underground. The granite at the bottom of the canyon was formed long before there were any people on earth, long before the days of the dinosaurs, even before the time when trilobites were the earth's leading animals. The story the canyon tells is a long chapter in the story of the earth.

A trip to the bottom of the canyon might also be called "Four Climates in a Mile's Journey." For traveling down into the canyon is like traveling from Canada to Mexico. Near the top one finds the blue spruces and aspens of Canada. Lower there are the

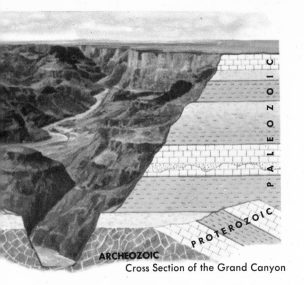
Cross Section of the Grand Canyon

yellow pines of the Rockies. Still lower one finds tree cacti like those of the southwest desert. At the bottom the plants are plants common in Mexico.

How did the Colorado River find its way into this great gash in the earth? The answer is that the river itself carved the valley. It had the help of many small but swift streams running into it. Nowhere else in the world is it so easy to see how running water can change the face of the earth. (See ARIZONA; EROSION; NATIONAL PARKS.)

GRAPES Vineyards, where grapes are grown, have been common for many centuries. The Bible mentions them. Probably the grape was one of the very first fruits men learned to raise.

Today there are more than 2,000 kinds of grapes. They have all come either from the wild grapes of the Near East or from those of North America. The picture shows a few of the many kinds.

Grapes grow on vines. The vines can be cut back till they are like bushes. But in most vineyards the vines are given wire fences to grow on. Even when the vines are on fences they are trimmed every year. Trimming them makes them bear better.

Some grapes are raised for raisins. Raisins are simply dried grapes. Some grapes are raised to be eaten in hand. Some are raised to be made into grape juice or jelly or jam. And a very great many are raised for wine. Making wine from grapes goes back many centuries.

In the grape-growing region near the Great Lakes many of the grapes grown are Concords. In Concord, Mass., there is a monument to the first Concord grapevine. This vine grew from a seed that was planted by accident. It probably was a seed of the wild fox grape, but its grapes were different from any other grape and were very good. All the other thousands of Concord grapevines have come from cuttings from this first Concord vine.

The greatest enemy of vineyards is a disease of the roots of the grapevine. Early settlers in America brought grapevines with them from Europe, but this root disease soon killed the vines. The disease was carried back across the ocean. Many vineyards in Europe were almost ruined. Then it was found that the wild grapes of America do not have this disease. Now many European vineyards have vines that have been grafted on to American roots. (See FRANCE; FRUITS; VINES.)

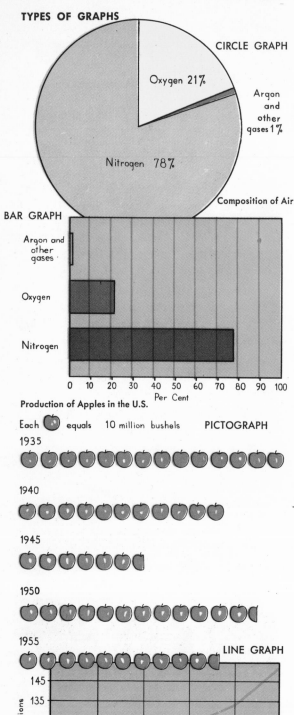

TYPES OF GRAPHS

CIRCLE GRAPH

Oxygen 21%

Argon and other gases 1%

Nitrogen 78%

Composition of Air

BAR GRAPH

Argon and other gases

Oxygen

Nitrogen

0 10 20 30 40 50 60 70 80 90 100
Per Cent

Production of Apples in the U.S.

Each ⚫ equals 10 million bushels   PICTOGRAPH

1935

1940

1945

1950

1955

LINE GRAPH

145
135
125
115
105
95
85
75

Population in millions

1900 1910 1920 1930 1940 1950

Growth of U.S. Population

GRAPHS The air is made up of many gases. But there are different amounts of these gases. Almost four-fifths of the air is nitrogen. A little more than one-fifth is oxygen. Argon and all the other gases together make up only about a hundredth of the air.

Each of the top two diagrams at the left tells all that the paragraph above tells. The diagrams are simpler ways of telling the story. Diagrams of such kinds are called graphs. The top graph is a circle graph. The second is a bar graph.

There are many kinds of graphs. Two other kinds are shown. The one with the pictures of apples is a pictograph. The other is a line graph. Isn't it easy to read the stories they tell?

GRASSES If there were no plants, there could be no animals. For all animals get their food from plants. They do not all eat plants. They may eat animals that eat plants. Or they may eat animals that eat animals that eat plants. But the food of every animal can be traced back to plants. We ourselves would have no food except salt and water if there were no plants.

Almost every plant is good food for some animal. For us the most important food plants are the grasses. Our bread and cereal grains—rice, corn, wheat, rye, barley, oats, and millet—are all grasses. So is sugar cane. So are the pasture grasses that feed our cows and sheep.

Some grasses are low plants. Some are middle-sized. And one grass—bamboo—is a tree. All grasses have jointed stems.

Grasses do more than give us food. They make beautiful lawns. They keep soil from washing away. They help build up good soil. In some parts of the world people

Wheat   Corn   Barley   Oats

The rapid spinning of the earth would throw everything off into space if it weren't for gravity.

make roofs or even whole houses of grass.

Although it would be hard to get along without the grass family, some grasses are weeds. Among them are crab grass and quack grass. (See BAMBOO; BREAD; CEREALS; CORN; FLOUR; FLOWER FAMILIES; FORAGE CROPS; PRAIRIE; RICE; RYE; SUGAR; WHEAT.)

GRAVITY Even a champion high-jumper can jump only about seven feet off the ground. The earth pulls him so hard that he cannot jump any higher. The pull of the earth is called gravity.

Gravity makes water run downhill. It makes balls thrown into the air fall back down, and ripe apples drop from trees. Gravity keeps us all from being hurled off the earth as it whirls around.

A person can easily find out how hard the earth is pulling him. All he has to do is weigh himself. If it weren't for gravity, no one would weigh anything at all.

It is fun to imagine getting away from the earth and taking a trip far out into space. Before anyone really can, however, some kind of space ship must be invented that will go fast enough to escape the earth's gravity. Scientists with their work on rockets and satellites will probably make possible in the near future real journeys into space. (See NEWTON, ISAAC.)

GREAT BRITAIN There are two big islands in the British Isles—Great Britain and Ireland. Great Britain is the larger of the two. England, Scotland, and Wales are on this island.

Great Britain is not much larger than Minnesota. But more than 15 times as many people live there. (See BRITISH EMPIRE; BRITISH ISLES; ENGLAND; SCOTLAND; UNITED KINGDOM; WALES.)

GREAT LAKES The Great Lakes are really great. Nowhere else is there such a chain of large lakes. Five lakes make up the chain. Each one of them is among the 15 biggest lakes in the world.

Lake Superior is the largest of the five. It is almost exactly the same size as the state of Maine. After Superior come Huron, Michigan, Erie, and Ontario.

Lake Michigan is entirely inside the United States. The other four are a part of the boundary that runs between the United States and Canada.

In Chicago there is a beautiful fountain called "The Spirit of the Great Lakes." It has a figure to stand for each one of the lakes. Superior and Michigan pour their water into Huron's bowl. Huron empties her bowl into Erie's. Erie, in turn, empties hers into Ontario's.

The water in the Great Lakes is fresh. Many rivers bring water to them. The St. Lawrence River carries water from Lake Ontario to the Atlantic.

There was a time during the Ice Age when the Great Lakes drained down the Mississippi Valley to the Gulf of Mexico. The valley of the St. Lawrence was blocked by ice. Now a little of the water once more finds its way to the Gulf through a waterway. But most of the water flows eastward. On its way between Lake Erie and Lake Ontario it pours over Niagara Falls.

The Great Lakes have helped to make the United States and Canada great countries. The lakes form a waterway more than 1,000 miles long. No other inland water-

way in the world is so busy. Many of the boats that travel the lakes are loaded with wheat, iron ore, and coal. Several Great Lakes ports are very large cities.

Canals have been dug to improve the lakes as a waterway. The "Soo" canals carry traffic between Superior and Huron. The Welland Canal lets boats pass Niagara Falls. The new St. Lawrence Seaway, which was opened in 1958, allows large ocean-going vessels to reach the lakes.

The lakes affect the climate of all the region around them. Near their shores there are thousands of orchards and vineyards. The lakes help make the climate good for fruit. They do much to make the climate pleasanter to live in, too.

Of course, the lakes give the people near them a wonderful chance to go sailing and fishing and swimming. In many places there are excellent beaches. No one could possibly measure in dollars how much the lakes are worth to the people who live near by. (See CANALS; CHICAGO; DETROIT; ICE AGE; LAKES; NIAGARA FALLS; ST. LAWRENCE RIVER.)

GREAT SALT LAKE The largest lake in the western half of the United States is Great Salt Lake. This lake is very different from the Great Lakes. For one thing, it is very shallow. On the average it is less than 15 feet deep. Besides, its water is very salty.

This lake is left over from a much bigger one—Lake Bonneville. Lake Bonneville once covered most of what is now the state of Utah. It was a great fresh-water lake 1,000 feet deep. Water poured into it down the slopes of surrounding mountains. Through a gap in the mountains overflow water found a way to the sea.

But in time the climate of the region became much drier. Less water ran into the lake, and much that did evaporated. Finally the lake was losing more water each year than it got. Of course, the lake became shallower and smaller. At last no water ran out of it to the sea. The lake grew salty, for the

water as it evaporated left behind the salt it had gathered up from rocks on its way to the lake. Now the water is much saltier than sea water. The only living things in Great Salt Lake are brine shrimps and tiny algae. Swimming in such salty water is a strange experience. The water holds a swimmer up much more than fresh water does. If he floats, a third of his body is out of water. Diving is rather dangerous. A diver may be stunned when he hits the heavy water.

Along the northwest shore of the lake are the Bonneville Salt Flats. "Flats" is a good name for them, for they are probably flatter than any other natural surface on the earth. The ground is almost pure salt. On the Flats there is an automobile racecourse. A racing car has traveled nearly 400 miles an hour on it.

Salt Lake City is near Great Salt Lake. Some of the people of the city earn their living by mining salt. Lake Bonneville left behind enough salt to last the whole world for a thousand years.

The best way to get a good view of the lake is to fly over it. On a sunshiny day the very blue lake with its border of salt makes a picture it is not easy to forget. (See ALGAE; CASPIAN SEA; SALT; UTAH.)

604

GREECE

Bust of Socrates

View of Acropolis

Chariot

Treading Grapes

Statue: Discus Thrower by Myron

Statue: Venus

Drinking Cup

Woman Weaving

Market Place

Women at Public Fountain

GREECE The world of today owes a great deal to the ancient Greeks. From them came much of our learning. They gave us many of our ideas of beauty, too, and the idea of democracy.

About 3,800 years ago a people moved into the mountainous peninsula of Greece, the western rim of Asia Minor, and hundreds of islands that dot the Aegean (e GEE an) Sea. They settled in small valleys separated by hills or mountains. Each community had a fort on a low hill and below it a

town of mud-brick houses. On small farms outside each town farmers grew wheat and barley and tended vineyards and olive orchards. They pastured their flocks and herds on valley slopes. These settlements became united into small kingdoms that lasted until about 1100 B.C. Homer's story-poems tell of the Trojan War and of other events in the days of the Greek kingdoms.

A period which is called the Dark Age of Greece then came. It ended as the period of classical Greece began.

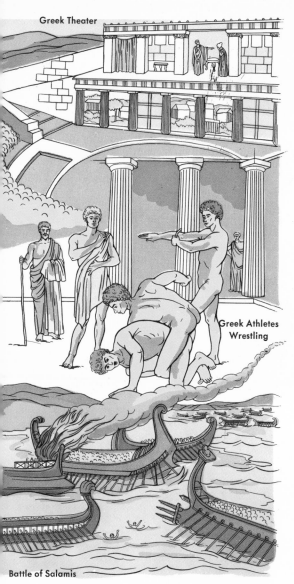

Greek Theater

Greek Athletes Wrestling

Battle of Salamis

copied the idea of silver coins, too. Writing and money helped Greek business.

The Greeks soon had better ships than the Phoenicians and went ahead of them in sea trade. By 600 B.C. Greek trading posts and colonies stretched along the northern Mediterranean shore from the Black Sea almost to the Atlantic. One of the most successful colonies was Syracuse in Sicily.

Workshops employing slave workmen made beautiful pottery, textiles, and metal wares for trade with other lands. The Greek ships brought home much grain and fish. Shipbuilders built warships to protect the merchant fleets. Merchants and workshop owners grew wealthy.

In Athens these newly wealthy men compelled the ruling nobles to share the government with them and with all the citizens. By 500 B.C. the Athenians had set up a democratic government. All free men could take part in the Assembly, the lawmaking body of the city-state. The Assembly sat on the grass in an open-air meeting place. Members voted by raising their hands.

Then arose a great threat to liberty. Xerxes, the powerful king of Persia, sent his armies by land and sea against Athens. In the Battle of Marathon in 490 B.C. the united "Greek spears" led by Athens defeated the "Persian bows and arrows." In the sea battle of Salamis in 480 B.C. the Athenians defeated the Persian navy.

After the Persian war the Athenians entered a Golden Age. They rebuilt their city, burned down by the Persians. Their new homes were still of mud brick, but they contained beautiful furnishings. Boys went to school at their teacher's house, attended by an old slave, the "pedagogue." He carried their roll books. Greek boys studied music, reading, writing, and poetry. Girls stayed at home. Young men practiced boxing, wrestling, and running in order to prepare for the famous Olympic games.

On a hill called the Acropolis the Athenians built a majestic marble temple—the Parthenon. It honored the goddess Athena,

In classical times each town with its farmland was called a city-state. There were many city-states, but the chief ones were Athens, Sparta, Corinth, and Thebes.

With the great sea at their door, the Greeks became a sea-trading people. They learned about trade from black-bearded Phoenician traders from across the Aegean and the Mediterranean. Greek nobles bought from them jewelry for their wives and robes dyed with beautiful Tyrian purple. From the Phoenicians, too, they learned about the alphabet and borrowed it for writing their own language. They

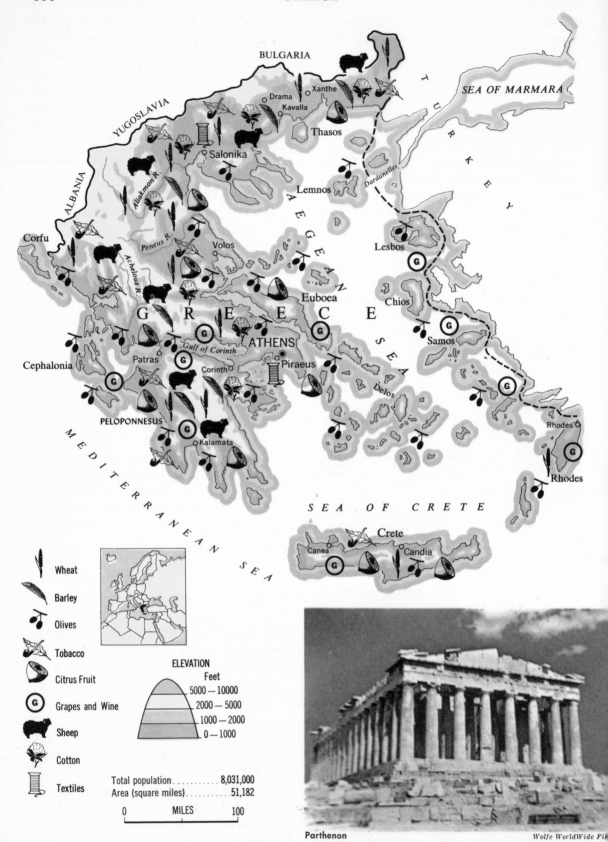

BULGARIA

SEA OF MARMARA

YUGOSLAVIA

Drama
Xanthe
Kavalla

Thasos

Salonika

TURKEY

Dardanelles

ALBANIA

Lemnos

A E G E A N

Corfu

Peneus R.

Volos

Achelous R.

Aliakmon R.

Lesbos

G

Chios

G

Samos

G R E E C E

Euboea

Cephalonia

Patras
Gulf of Corinth
ATHENS
Corinth
Piraeus

G
G

G

S E A

Delos

G

PELOPONNESUS

Kalamata

G

Rhodes

G

M E D I T E R R A N E A N S E A

Rhodes

SEA OF CRETE

Crete
Canea
Candia
G

Legend:

- Wheat
- Barley
- Olives
- Tobacco
- Citrus Fruit
- G Grapes and Wine
- Sheep
- Cotton
- Textiles

ELEVATION
Feet
5000 — 10000
2000 — 5000
1000 — 2000
0 — 1000

Total population 8,031,000
Area (square miles) 51,182

0   MILES   100

Parthenon

the protector of Athens. The young leader Pericles planned it; Phidias, the most famous sculptor of his time, carved its marvelous decorations.

Many men of learning arose in the Golden Age. Sophocles and Euripides wrote plays for the open-air theater below the Acropolis. The great teachers Socrates and Plato held conversations with young citizens in the market place. Modern medicine started with the physician Hippocrates (hi POK ra teez). Aristotle argued that the earth is round 1800 years before the time of Columbus.

The Golden Age faded. Rivalry brought on wars between the city-states. From the north, Alexander the Great, king of Macedonia, led his armies into Greece. He made the Greek city-states a part of his empire. Alexander did not think much of democracy, but he liked Greek art and learning. Throughout his empire he spread Greek architecture, sculpture, and science. Much later the Romans, who conquered Alexander's empire, carried Greek ideas to western Europe. From Europe, in time, these ideas reached the New World.

Greece won her independence from Turkey in 1830. For most of the time since then she has been a kingdom. The period of World War II and the next few years were troubled ones for the small country.

Most of the people of Greece today get their living from the soil and the sea just as the ancient Greeks did. Very little manufacturing goes on.

Unfortunately there are so many mountains and lakes in Greece that only one-fourth of the country's area can be used for fields and orchards. And during the centuries much of the soil has been worn out. Almost all the forests, moreover, have been cut down. But Greece is replanting her forests and rebuilding her soil.

Like all the countries on the northern shores of the Mediterranean, Greece has a good climate for olives, citrus fruits, grapes, and figs. Olive oil and the small dried grapes called currants are among her exports. The farmers have some livestock —chiefly sheep and goats.

From the sea the fishermen get sponges. And as in days of long ago Greek ships carry cargoes far over the seas. The people of only two nations in the world own more merchant ships than the Greeks.

Athens, the capital of Greece, attracts many visitors. It still has signs of Greece's early glory. (See ALEXANDER THE GREAT; ARCHIMEDES; ARISTOTLE; DEMOCRACY; GREEK MYTHS; HISTORY; HOMER; OLYMPIC GAMES; PERSIA; PHOENICIANS; ROME, ANCIENT; SOCRATES; TROJAN WAR.)

Sheepherders

Olives

Greek Flag

Mt. Olympus

Greek
Royal Guard

Galatea

Daedalus

Icarus

Pygmalion

Medea

Jason

Pandora

Theseus and
the Minotaur

GREEK MYTHS Back near the beginning of things, an old Greek story goes, there was only one woman on the earth. Her name was Pandora. The gods had sent her down to earth from Mt. Olympus, their home, to be the wife of Epimetheus. As she was leaving Mt. Olympus, Zeus, the king of the gods, had given her a golden casket. He had commanded her never to open it.

For a time Pandora obeyed the order. But one day she grew so curious that she decided to take just one peek. As she lifted the lid, a swarm of horrid little creatures flew out. They flew about stinging people and making them cry with anger and pain. No one could catch them to put them back in the box. Up to that time there had been no sickness or sorrow on the earth. Pan-

dora, unhappy about the harm she had done, looked once more into the casket. Now she saw a beautiful gem. It was Hope.

A story of this kind is called a myth. There are many other Greek myths. The Greeks made them up to explain things they could not understand. They told the story of Pandora to explain why there is sickness and sorrow and why there is always hope that the world will become better.

The myths of the Greeks were closely tied up with their religion. In most of them their gods and goddesses play an important part. The pictures show some of the characters in these myths.

With the help of the gods, the young man Bellerophon captured Pegasus, the winged horse of the Muses. Together Bellerophon and Pegasus performed heroic deeds. But when Bellerophon tried to ride Pegasus up to Mt. Olympus, he was thrown off. Pegasus returned alone to his home with the gods.

Theseus killed the Minotaur, a monster that devoured seven Greek youths and seven Greek maidens each year. After killing the monster, Theseus escaped from a great maze, or labyrinth.

Orpheus, who played wonderful music on his lyre, was allowed to go to Hades to bring back his dead wife Eurydice (you RID i see). But on the way out of Hades he disobeyed a command of the gods and looked back to be sure that Eurydice was following. She then disappeared forever.

Icarus, while wearing wings, disobeyed his father Daedalus and flew too close to the sun. The wax of the wings melted and Icarus plunged into the sea.

Perseus cut off the head of the Gorgon Medusa, the sight of whom turned people to stone. He also rescued the beautiful maiden Andromeda from a sea monster.

Medea helped Jason secure the Golden Fleece. Pygmalion, a sculptor, fell in love with Galatea, a statue he had made. In answer to his prayers the goddess of love brought the statue to life.

Hercules was given 12 labors to perform. One was to capture the sacred stag belonging to Artemis, the goddess of the hunt. He did so by running after it day and night for a whole year.

The gods gave Atalanta the gift of fleetness. She promised to marry any young man who could outrun her. But anyone who tried and failed was put to death. The goddess of love gave Hippomenes three golden apples. During the race he flung them, one at a time, ahead of Atalanta. She stooped to pick them up and lost the race.

Many Greek myths are nature myths. They explain such things as what holds up the earth, why the seasons change, and how the different groups of stars came to be in the sky. Such nature myths can be called the forerunners of science. (See AMBROSIA; ANIMALS, FABULOUS; BOSPORUS; CONSTELLATIONS; CRETE; FATES; HADES; MYTHS AND LEGENDS; ORACLES; TROJAN WAR.)

Bellerophon

Andromeda

Perseus

Pegasus

Medusa's Head

Sea Monster

Danaë and the Shower of Gold

Atalanta

Hippomenes

Orpheus Weeping for Eurydice

Hercules and Artemis' Stag

HORACE GREELEY

GREELEY, HORACE (1811-1872) Newspapers have played an important part in America's history. Some of them, of course, have been much more important than others. How much power a newspaper has depends chiefly on how good an editor it has. Horace Greeley is one of the most famous of all American newspaper editors.

Greeley did not have much education. He went to work in a printing office when he was only 14. He was the kind of helper called a "printer's devil." It was not long before Greeley decided that he wanted to run a newspaper of his own. He and a friend went to New York and started one. It lasted only three weeks. Soon afterward Greeley started another newspaper. It did not last either. But then he started the *Daily Tribune*. This paper was such a success that it lasted for 83 years until it merged with the *Herald* in 1924.

In his newspaper Greeley fought against slavery. He fought against saloons. He also fought against letting women vote. Not all of Greeley's ideas were good, but he thought that they were and worked hard to bring others to his way of thinking.

People would not have taken the trouble to read Greeley's ideas if they had had to read them in his handwriting. His writing was so poor that it could truthfully be said that it looked like chicken tracks.

Greeley's advice "Go West, young man, go West," became famous all over the United States. Greeley made a trip to the western part of the country and was so pleased with what he saw that he decided the West held the greatest promise for the future. (See NEWSPAPERS; PRINTING.)

GREENHOUSE Glass houses built to protect growing plants are called greenhouses. The glass allows sunlight in, and then keeps the heat of the sunlight from escaping. A caretaker supplies water and good soil so that plants have everything they need for growing.

One good reason for having greenhouses is that plants can be started in them early in the spring while it is still cold out of doors. When it is warm enough and there is no longer danger of frost, the plants can be transplanted from their home under glass to the garden. Tomatoes and cabbage are two vegetables which are often started early in spring under glass.

Greenhouses also help make it possible for us to have flowers and fresh vegetables all through the year. In the seasons when there are no plants growing in outdoor gardens, a greenhouse owner can sell flowers or vegetables from his greenhouse.

Many experiments are done with plants in greenhouses, too. From these experiments scientists have found out a great deal about what plants need in order to grow well. They have also found out a great deal about plant diseases.

In some parts of the world people would never see orchids or banana plants or giant ferns if there were no greenhouses. Greenhouses can display plants that are very different from those growing naturally around us. (See ORCHIDS; PLANT BREEDING; PLANT FACTORIES.)

Flowers bloom the year round in greenhouses.

Most of the people of Greenland are Eskimos.

GREENLAND The world's biggest island is Greenland. It is far to the north, between North America and Europe. Its northernmost point is nearer the North Pole than any other land we know about.

In spite of its size there are not enough people in Greenland to make one good-sized city. There are less than 25,000 people on the whole island. Most of them are Eskimos. But a few hundred are Danes. The island belongs to Denmark.

Most of Greenland is covered by a great icecap. In the center the ice is more than a mile deep. Only a few bare rocky peaks stick up through this thick sheet of ice. There is only a narrow strip of ice-free land around the edges of the island where people can live. In some places the ice comes all the way down to the sea.

The Eskimos of Greenland live as Eskimos in other places do. Most of the Danish people in Greenland live along the southern edge. But even the southern edge is farther north than Labrador. One Danish post office in Greenland is farther north than any other post office in the world.

There are important weather stations in Greenland. Their reports help the weathermen of Europe and America forecast the weather. Greenland is becoming more important as a stopping place for planes flying across the Arctic. Arctic air routes are the shortest routes between northern North America and northern Europe and Asia. (See AIRWAYS; DENMARK; ESKIMOS; U.S. WEATHER BUREAU.)

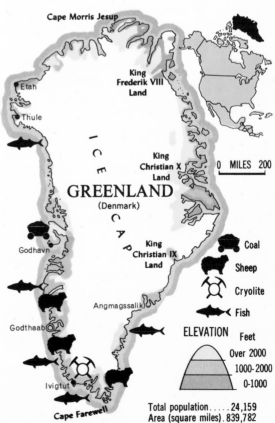

Cape Morris Jesup

Etah

Thule

King Frederik VIII Land

King Christian X Land

0   MILES   200

GREENLAND
(Denmark)

King Christian IX Land

Godhavn

Angmagssalik

Godthaab

Ivigtut

Cape Farewell

Coal

Sheep

Cryolite

Fish

ELEVATION   Feet

Over 2000
1000-2000
0-1000

Total population.....24,159
Area (square miles).839,782

Two strong teams of horses could not pull von Guericke's ball apart.

GUERICKE (GAY ri ke), **OTTO VON** (1602-1686) About 300 years ago a German scientist sent word to his emperor that he wished to show him an experiment. The scientist was Otto von Guericke. The picture at the top of the page shows the experiment. The big ball is a hollow ball made in two halves that are not fastened together. With an air pump he had invented, von Guericke pumped out most of the air from inside the ball. Then the air on the outside held the two halves together. It pushed on them with so much force that strong horses could not pull them apart.

In many science classes today boys and girls try this same experiment. But the balls they use are only a few inches across. The balls are called Magdeburg hemispheres. They get this name because von Guericke was the mayor of the city of Magdeburg.

Von Guericke carried on many other experiments. He experimented with electricity and invented a machine for producing sparks of electricity. He studied winds and weather and built a water barometer.

This water barometer had a glass tube more than 30 feet tall that reached up through the roof of von Guericke's house. The tube was almost filled with water. A little wooden figure floated on the water. On clear days the water rose, and the little figure appeared above the roof. On cloudy days the water went down in the tube, and the little figure disappeared below the roof. The neighbors did not understand a barometer. When they saw the little figure appear and disappear, they said that von Guericke was in league with the devil. It was not easy to be a scientist 300 years ago. (See AIR; BAROMETER.)

GUIANAS Three little countries on the northern coast of South America are called the Guianas. They are Netherlands Guiana, British Guiana, and French Guiana. Another name for Netherlands Guiana is Surinam. Back in the days when the American colonies were first being settled, the Netherlands traded New Netherland (New York) to the British for Surinam.

There is some beautiful scenery in the Guianas. But not many people see it. The lowland along the Guiana coast is hot, rainy, and uncomfortable to live in. Most land in the Guianas is high, rugged, and covered with dense forests. These countries are not on any main steamship or airline route. And they have few roads and almost no railroads.

Most people in the Guianas live in the lowland. Among them are native Indians and some Europeans. Their homes are in the cities or on sugar, rice, and other plantations. Europeans have brought in many

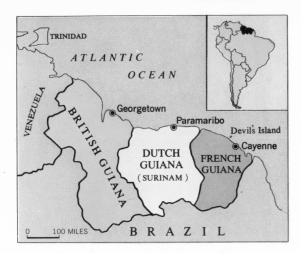

GULF OF MEXICO The Gulf of Mexico is a big arm of the Atlantic Ocean. Five of the southern states of the United States have seacoasts on the Gulf. They are Florida, Alabama, Mississippi, Louisiana, and Texas. Mexico has more than 1,000 miles of Gulf coast.

The Mississippi River flows into the Gulf of Mexico. New Orleans, one of the two great Gulf ports, is near the mouth of the Mississippi. The other great Gulf port is Houston, Texas.

Warm winds often blow from the Gulf over the eastern half of the United States. These winds bring much rain to that part of the country. From time to time hurricanes sweep across the Gulf and do damage to the coastal regions. Galveston, Texas, was almost destroyed in 1900.

The Gulf is a busy highway. Ships go between its ports and ports all over the world. Many of these ships are oil tankers or fruit boats. Others carry cotton, sulfur, or chemicals. Some are passenger ships. Many of the ships which leave Gulf ports are bound for South America. (See MEXICO; MISSISSIPPI RIVER; NEW ORLEANS.)

Negroes from Africa and many people from the East Indies to work on the plantations. In earlier times France used Devil's Island as a colony for convicts.

Near streams in the forests there are scattered Indian villages and villages of Negroes who ran away from plantations. The village people travel in canoes. They raise a little food and catch fish. Often they shoot the fish with bows and arrows.

The United States gets much aluminum ore from Surinam. That ore is called bauxite. It is used in American aluminum plants.

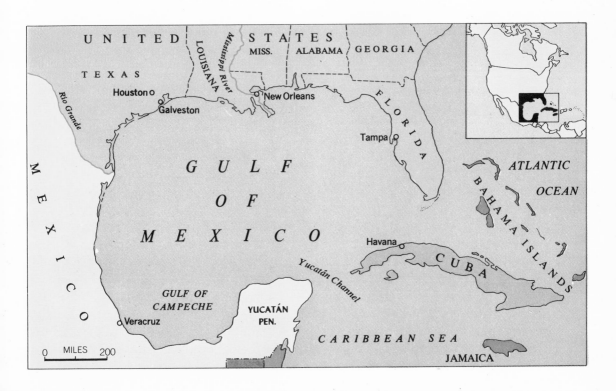

GULF STREAM In the oceans there are great "rivers" called ocean currents. The Gulf Stream is the largest and most important of these ocean currents.

The Gulf Stream is a current of warm water which flows out from the Gulf of Mexico between Florida and Cuba. For a way it travels along the east coast of the United States. Then it swings eastward in the Atlantic Ocean.

As it leaves the Gulf it is a very blue stream of water 100 miles wide and several hundred feet deep—far larger than the Mississippi River. And it is traveling fast —often more than 100 miles a day. It slows down as it moves northward.

The Gulf Stream is often 20° warmer than the water beside it. Its western edge is called the "cold wall." Winds blowing across the Gulf Stream carry some of its warmth to the countries of northern Europe. England is as far north as Labrador, but partly because of the Gulf Stream its climate is much pleasanter. (See ATLANTIC OCEAN; CLIMATE; OCEANS.)

Gutenberg cast movable type.

GUTENBERG, JOHANN (1400?-1468) One of the most famous books in the world is the Gutenberg Bible. As much as half a million dollars has been paid for a single copy of it. It gets its name because Johann Gutenberg is supposed to have printed it. But probably an early printer named Schoeffer printed it instead.

Gutenberg is often called the inventor of printing. Most people, when they talk about the invention of printing, mean

printing with separate type letters. But Gutenberg probably did not invent printing of this kind. The Chinese are believed to have printed from clay letters long before. Nothing, however, came of their invention. Printing was invented over again in Europe. No one is sure who invented it in Europe. Probably the inventor kept his invention secret because he wanted buyers to think his books had been done by hand.

But even if Gutenberg did not print the Gutenberg Bible or invent printing, he deserves his fame. He devised a way of casting the metal letters to be used. He used brass molds to make very beautiful and usable type. He took the ideas of others and worked out improvements that helped greatly in making printing what it is today. (See BIBLE; BOOKS AND BOOKBINDING; NEWSPAPERS; PRINTING.)

GYMNASTICS The word "gymnastics" comes from the same old Greek word that "gymnasium" comes from. The word meant "naked." Gymnastics are exercises meant to make the body strong. Greek gymnasts wore no clothing as they exercised.

The pictures show some common gymnastic exercises. In college meets champions are chosen in each of these exercises.

The people of many countries are interested in gymnastics. The gymnasts of Sweden are famous. They do not use any apparatus. Teams from Sweden have come to the United States many times to show their skill. (See ATHLETICS; GREECE; OLYMPIC GAMES.)

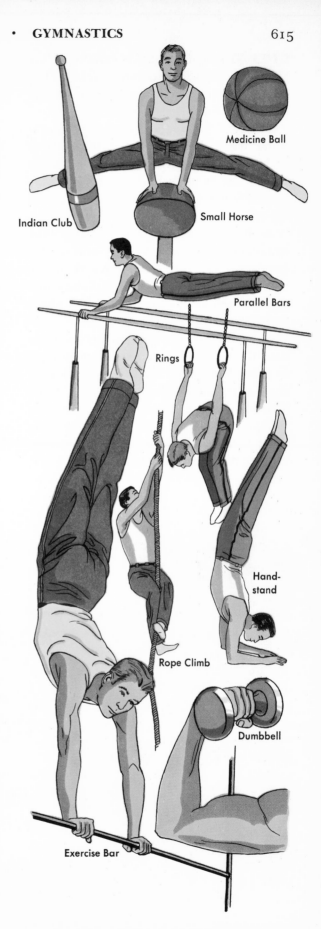

Medicine Ball

Indian Club

Small Horse

Parallel Bars

Rings

Hand-stand

Rope Climb

Dumbbell

Exercise Bar

GYPSIES Fortunetellers are often dressed as gypsies. Sometimes they are real gypsies. For telling fortunes is one of the chief ways in which gypsies, wherever they are, make a living.

Gypsies are nomads. They wander about from place to place. No one knows much about their early story. About 600 years ago tribes of gypsies wandered into Europe from Asia. Perhaps in the beginning they came from India. They are dark-skinned and black-haired like the people of India. And their language makes scientists think that they came from India. But the early gypsies said that they came from Egypt. "Gypsies" is short for "Egyptians."

In Europe the gypsies kept on wandering, moving northward in summer and southward in winter. They traveled in wagons pulled by horses. At night they built big campfires and sang songs around them.

The gypsies were soon famous for their horse trading and their fortunetelling. Some of them were good smiths, too. Some earned money by mending pots and pans. And some were good musicians. Many composers have used gypsy tunes in their music.

The lives of the gypsies seemed to be very happy and carefree. Many other people wished that they could live as easy a life. But the gypsies were not always well treated. They sometimes had to steal to get enough food. People began to be afraid of them. They were even driven out of some countries for a time.

From Europe some of the gypsies wandered to the Americas and to Australia. In all their wanderings they have kept very much to themselves. They also cling to their own customs and their own language. Their language is called Romany.

There are thousands of gypsies in the United States now. As they wander about they now usually use automobiles instead of horses and wagons. Many of them spend the winters in cities. With their gay clothes and bright jewelry they are easy to tell from other people. (See NOMADS.)

GYROSCOPE A toy gyroscope spins like a top. In fact, this toy is often called a gyrotop. The chief parts of the gyrotop are a wheel which is weighted around the rim and a rod, or axle, that goes through the center of the wheel. In spinning a gyrotop, a string is first wrapped around the axle. Then the string is pulled suddenly as the end of the axle is rested on something solid. Once a gyrotop starts spinning it does not change its position until it runs down. Its axle keeps on pointing in the same direction. It can remain in amazing positions as it spins. The whirling of the heavy wheel keeps it from falling.

Not all gyroscopes are toys. Some are used in boats as compasses. Some are used to keep boats and airplanes on a straight course. A gyroscope used in this way is called a gyropilot. One nickname for a gyropilot is "metal Mike." In fighting at sea during a war gyroscopes are used to guide torpedoes. On some ships enormous gyroscopes are used to help keep the ships on an even keel so that passengers will not be seasick.

Only toy gyroscopes are set to spinning by the pulling of a string. As a rule other gyroscopes are set in motion and kept spinning with electricity. (See COMPASS.)

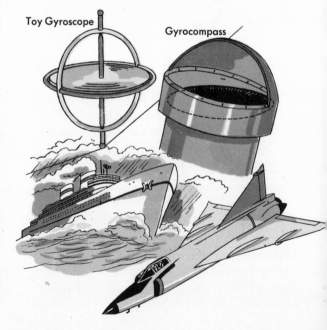

Toy Gyroscope

Gyrocompass

The letter *H* can be traced back to this letter in the Phoenician alphabet (目). In the beginning the letter may have come from the same picture that *E* came from—the picture of a man praying or shouting for joy. Some scholars think that it came instead from the picture of a fence or of a lotus flower. The Greeks simplified the letter after they borrowed it from the Phoenicians (H). It has come down to us by way of the Romans unchanged.

H is pronounced in such words as hate, home, and hear, but in a great many words it is silent. Hour, honor, vehicle, and vehement are a few of them.

HABITS If we had to think of each step we took as we walked down the street, it would take us a long time to walk even one block. It would also take a great deal of time if we had to think carefully of each letter we made as we wrote our own names. We learn to walk and to write so well that walking and writing are habits.

We depend on a large number of habits when we dress in the morning. Tying bows,

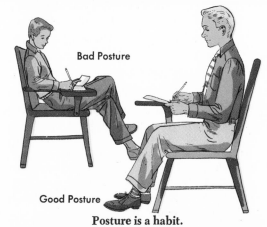

Bad Posture

Good Posture

Posture is a habit.

buttoning buttons, snapping snaps, and zipping zippers are all habits. Using knives and forks and spoons as we eat is a habit. Brushing our teeth after meals is a habit. Turning off lights when we leave a room and waiting for a green light at street corners are also habits. Our lives would not be at all as they are now if there were no such thing as habit and we had to think carefully about everything we do.

We form a habit by doing the same thing over and over again. But want and need have a great deal to do with forming habits. Walking would not become a habit if we felt no need or desire to walk.

Although habits are very important to us and most of them may be good, we may have some bad habits. Many people have formed the habit of standing or sitting in bad positions. Some people have the habit of biting their fingernails. Some have the habit of paying no attention to traffic lights at street crossings. Some people have formed bad eating habits. A long list of bad habits could easily be made.

If you are learning to do anything new, it is a good plan to make sure you are doing it the right way. It is usually easier to form a good habit than to break a bad one.

HADES The people of ancient Greece thought that the earth was flat. Down below it, they believed, there was a great, gloomy region to which people went when they died. This underworld the Greeks called Hades after the name of the god who ruled it. Pluto was another name for this god of the underworld.

In Hades there was supposed to be a wide river—the Styx. The spirits of the dead had to cross the River Styx to enter Hades. On the bank of the river an old boatman, Charon, was always waiting to row them across. A huge dog with many heads stood guard at the gate of Hades to keep anyone who entered the underworld from escaping. The name of this dog was Cerberus. (See GREEK MYTHS.)

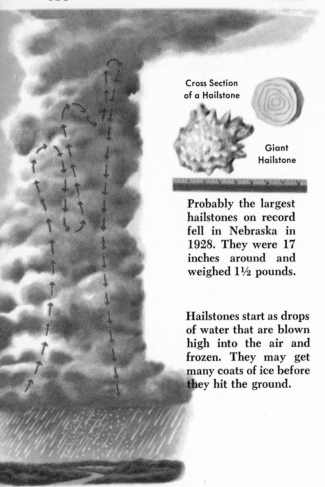

Cross Section
of a Hailstone

Giant
Hailstone

Probably the largest
hailstones on record
fell in Nebraska in
1928. They were 17
inches around and
weighed 1½ pounds.

Hailstones start as drops
of water that are blown
high into the air and
frozen. They may get
many coats of ice before
they hit the ground.

HAIL AND SLEET When raindrops start down from the clouds to the ground, they may fall into a layer of very cold air. If the air is cold enough, the raindrops freeze. When they reach the ground they are tiny balls of ice. These tiny balls of ice are called sleet. Sleet falls in late autumn, in winter, and in early spring. Oddly enough, much larger balls of ice often fall in the summer. We call these big balls of ice hail.

Hail usually falls during a thunderstorm. Even on hot summer days there may be a layer of very cold air only a mile or two above the ground. The top part of a thunderhead may be made up of snow crystals instead of drops of water. Hail is formed in thunderstorm clouds in this way: Raindrops formed in the lower part of the cloud are caught by air moving upward from the hot ground. They are blown up to the upper part of the cloud and are frozen. They get a coating of snow, too. They start to fall and get a coating of rain. But again the air catches them and blows them upward. The water freezes and the balls of ice get another coating of snow. Up they go time after time. When they are finally heavy enough to fall through the strong upcurrent of air, they may be as big as baseballs. Fortunately, few hailstones ever get to be that big.

Scientists know how hailstones are formed because they have cut them open. They are always made up of layers of clear ice and snowy ice. Sometimes there are as many as 25 layers of ice in one hailstone.

Hail can do a great deal of damage. The balls of ice are big enough to break the windows of greenhouses. They knock down fields of grain. They ruin flowers and tear leaves off trees and bushes. They may even kill chickens. It is a good thing that hail does not come with every thunderstorm. (See CLOUDS; RAIN; STORMS.)

HAIR A lamb's wool, a kitten's fur, and a little girl's curls are all hair. Only mammals, the animals that feed their babies with milk, have hair. They all have some, even though such mammals as whales, elephants, hippopotamuses, and rhinoceroses have only a few bristles.

A person has a covering of hair everywhere except on the palms of his hands and the soles of his feet. But over most of his body the hairs are too short and fine to show very clearly.

Under a microscope the hair of different animals may look quite different. The hair of different people may show very strong differences, too.

Most hair has some coloring matter, or pigment, in it. White hair has none.

Hair may be coarse or fine, thick or thin, straight or curly. But it all grows from the skin in the same way. Each hair has a "root." A small blood vessel brings food to the hair root. Otherwise the hair could not

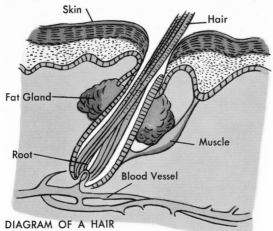

Skin
Hair
Fat Gland
Muscle
Root
Blood Vessel

DIAGRAM OF A HAIR

HALE, NATHAN (1755-1776) "I only regret that I have but one life to lose for my country." These words are famous as Nathan Hale's last words.

Nathan Hale was a young schoolteacher in Connecticut when the American Revolution began. He joined the American army at once as a lieutenant. He was such a good soldier that he was soon made a captain.

In 1776 Washington had been defeated in the Battle of Long Island and things looked dark for him and his troops. He needed to know more about what the British were planning to do. He asked someone to volunteer for the dangerous task of going back of the British lines to find out what was going on. Nathan Hale offered to go.

Hale's friends tried to persuade him not to go. He was so popular and so capable, they said, that he would be missed too much if he were lost. But he went.

grow. At each root there is a tiny muscle. There is also a tiny nerve. When hair "stands on end," the nerve has brought a message to the muscle and the muscle has pulled the hair into a stand-up position. Little oil glands in the skin constantly keep the hair oiled.

A covering of hair is a good protection. It shuts in the heat of an animal's body. It also helps keep the animal's body from being injured.

The hair of other animals is very useful to us. Fur coats are made of the skin and hair of other animals. Cloth and rugs are made from the hair of animals, especially from the wool of sheep. Many brushes are made of animal bristles. (See CARPETS AND RUGS; FURS; WOOL.)

By pretending that he was a Dutch schoolteacher, he got through the British lines. Soon he had a great deal of information for Washington. But on his way back to the American camp he was caught.

The British followed the rules of war and hanged him. To them he was just a spy. But to the Americans he was, and still is, a great patriot. Many statues have been erected in honor of this hero.

Hale's last words have inspired many Americans.

HALLOWEEN The night of October 31 is Halloween. The word "Halloween" is short for "Allhallows' evening." "Hallow" means "saint." The evening gets its name because the next day, November 1, is a church festival called All Saints' Day.

But the things we do to celebrate Halloween have nothing to do with the church. They have come down to us from early days in Britain. In those days, October 31 was the last day of the year there. It was a time for fun much like the fun we now have on New Year's Eve. On the night of October 31 witches and ghosts and goblins were supposed to be about, too.

Jack-o'-lanterns are one of the commonest signs of Halloween now. But witches and ghosts and black cats are also used a great deal for Halloween decorations. Many Halloween games are rather spooky.

HAMSTER The friendly, gentle little hamster has become popular with boys and girls as a pet. The hamsters now found in America are often called Syrian golden hamsters because they were originally found wild in Syria, and their color is usually a golden brown.

Their soft, fur-covered bodies are about five inches long and end with a stubby tail. They have black eyes, perky ears, and a queer little nose that appears to sniff all the time. In fact, a hamster looks very much like a small squirrel without a bushy tail. A hamster acts like a squirrel, too. It reminds one most of a squirrel when it sits up on its hind feet and gnaws grain which it holds with its front feet. It is not surprising that hamsters and squirrels look much alike, for they both belong to the big group of gnawing animals, or rodents.

Hamsters have roomy pouches, reaching back from their mouths to their shoulders, into which they cram food. The pouches can be seen only when they have food in them. Hamsters empty their pouches and store the food in their dens. They use their front feet much like hands when they fill and empty their pouches.

Their food consists chiefly of grains, vegetables, and fruits. Dry dog food in pellets, vegetable and fruit scraps, and corn make a good diet for hamster pets.

Wild hamsters are ground dwellers and carry on most of their activities at night. Pet hamsters can be kept in small wire cages with shredded paper or straw for a nest and containers for both food and water. They are orderly little animals and keep a clean, dry cage. They thrive best at ordinary room temperatures.

Hamster Eating Grain

Food Stored in Pouches

Baby Hamsters

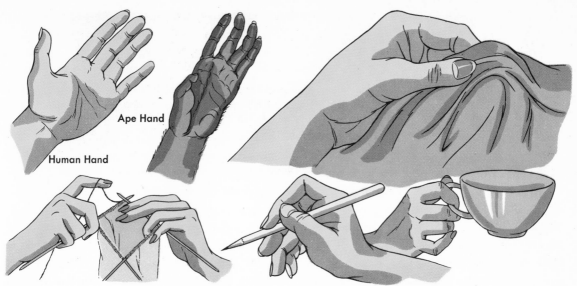

Ape Hand

Human Hand

The thumb makes it possible for the hand to clutch and hold.

Hamsters are grown up when they are two months old. One hamster mother may have from eight to fifteen babies in a litter. When the babies are about three weeks old they are able to care for themselves. The mother should then be separated from them and allowed to rest. After a week's rest she will be ready to mate and prepare for another family. The new family of babies will be born in about fifteen days.

Hamsters are not only good pets but good laboratory animals as well. They do not have many diseases of their own, but they can be given human diseases. They are becoming as useful in medical experiments as guinea pigs and white rats.

All the domestic hamsters in America are probably descended from a mother hamster and her twelve babies. This hamster family was found in a burrow near Aleppo, Syria, in 1930. Descendants from this family were brought to the United States in 1938. (See PETS; RODENTS.)

HAND In the days of our cave-man ancestors it did not seem that man had much of a chance to survive. He was not nearly as big or as strong as the giant cave bears and some of his other animal enemies. But he managed to hold his own. Today man is ruler of the earth.

We have been able to win out partly because we have a better brain than any other animal, and partly because we have good hands. With his brain early man could invent weapons for fighting, tools for building, and machines for helping him raise crops. With his hands early man could make and use the weapons and tools and machines he invented.

Many animals use their front feet as hands at times. Squirrels hold nuts as they eat them. Kangaroos can be taught to box. Kittens will play with a ball with their front paws. Apes have hands very much like ours. But no other animals use their hands as well as we do.

Each of our hands has four fingers and a thumb. The thumb is important. It can push in the opposite direction from the fingers and can thus help us hold things tightly. Many pairs of little muscles move our fingers and thumbs. They make it possible for us to do such things as sewing, writing, and piano playing.

With the ends of our fingers we can tell whether what we touch is hot or cold, rough or smooth, hard or soft. Our fingertips are very sensitive. Fortunately, we have nails that help protect them and that add to their usefulness. (See BODY, HUMAN; MAN; NAILS; SKELETON.)

Tugboats are needed to guide an ocean liner to its dock.

HARBORS AND PORTS Ocean vessels follow definite sea highways. There is a city at each end of a sea route. Such a city is called a seaport. One can see these ocean routes and their seaports on some world maps. One sees that many routes meet at cities like London and New York. At others few routes meet. Some coastal cities appear to have no routes at all. One may wonder, "Why do more routes and ships head for certain cities rather than for others?"

The great seaports of the world have, first, good harbors. A harbor is a sheltered body of water where ships may anchor. A good harbor is able to protect ships at anchor from stormy seas. It faces away from storm-bearing winds. It is deep enough so that the keels of large ships do not scrape the bottom. Its bed is not too rocky or too muddy for ships to anchor. A good harbor has room for ships to turn around and to pass one another. It has a deep, straight channel leading to the sea. Having no ice during the year also helps.

The land bordering the harbor should be level and firm enough to hold port buildings and equipment. Piers and docks where ships are loaded and unloaded line the harbors. Some harbors have special gates built to lock in the water at the docks when the tide goes out. These are called "lock docks." Warehouses, elevators, tracks, and streets

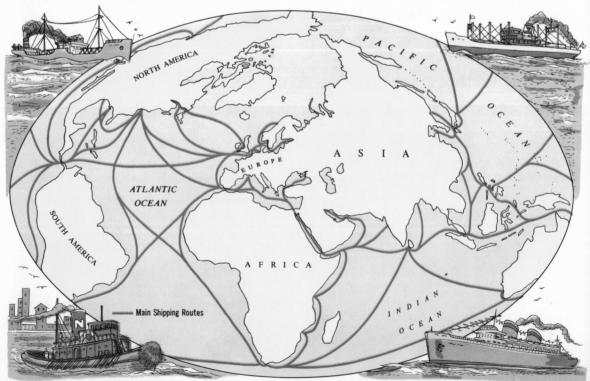

Main Shipping Routes

Harbors like this one provide protection for small boats, sailing vessels, and large ocean steamers. The high cliff shuts out strong storm winds from the ocean. The breakwater at the left keeps out rough waves. Many cities are on good harbors.

take up much space along the waterfront of a port.

Even good harbors differ from one another. The harbor of Rio de Janeiro, Brazil, is a wide bay protected by land on three sides. In some places deep, roomy river mouths called estuaries furnish good harbors. Such are the harbors of New York, Philadelphia, London, Hamburg, and Shanghai. If the port city is up the river some distance from the sea, like London, ocean vessels can carry their goods far inland before docking. This is often an advantage, because most water transportation costs less than rail or highway hauling.

Some good harbors are made by nature, but men must continually keep the channels deep and straight by dredging out sand and mud. Some harbors are entirely manmade. San Pedro, the port for Los Angeles, is on a man-made harbor. Long concrete breakwaters were built to make the harbor.

Most of the world's largest cities are seaports. But a good harbor alone is not enough to make a great seaport. A great port must have, second, a back country where many busy people are producing goods for export and where many thousands of people are able to buy foreign goods.

A great seaport must have, third, good connections with its back country by means of railroads, highways, or rivers. New York surpasses other Atlantic ports not because of a better harbor but partly because of better land connections with the rich interior of the United States.

Not all ports are seaports. Many cities on good lake harbors have become busy ports. A number of Great Lakes ports such as Chicago, Milwaukee, and Duluth are on harbors at the mouths of rivers. There are also river ports that serve river traffic. Duisburg-Hamborn, Germany, is such a port on the Rhine. Since river ports are not on harbors, as lake and seaports are, the river channel must be made wide enough for river boats or barges to dock.

Harbors and ports play an important part in bringing people and products together. (See CITIES; LAKES; OCEANS; RAILROADS; RIVERS; SHIPS; TRAMP STEAMER; TRANSPORTATION.)

UNCLE REMUS
CHARACTERS

Brer Rabbit
and Brer B'ar

Brer Wolf

Brer Rabbit

Brer Possum

The Deceitful Frog and Brer Fox

HARMONICA Two hundred years ago some of the great composers were writing music for a new instrument called the harmonica. Benjamin Franklin invented it. It was made of glass bowls. A player played the instrument by running his fingers around the rims of the bowls.

The harmonica of today is not at all the same. Other names for the kind now used are "mouth organ" and "French harp." The player blows into his harmonica and makes thin strips of metal called reeds move back and forth, or vibrate. The moving reeds produce the sound.

No one knows who invented the harmonica used today. It was brought to the United States from Europe more than 100 years ago. At first it was called an "aeolina" after the Greek god of the winds.

The harmonica is an easy instrument to play. There are harmonica bands in many schools. (See WIND INSTRUMENTS.)

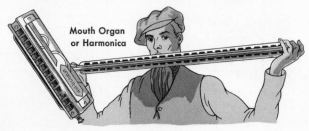

Mouth Organ
or Harmonica

HARRIS, JOEL CHANDLER (1848-1908) Some stories that are made up sound so real that we almost believe they are true. The wonderful tales of Uncle Remus, by Joel Chandler Harris, are such stories. They sound almost like things that really happened, even though they are about animals that can talk.

Harris was born in the small Georgia town of Eatontown. As a boy he was always fond of games and of animals. But often he liked to sit quietly and listen to people talk. He had a very good memory for the way people talked and the things they said.

When he was still a boy, Joel started to work on a newspaper as a printer's helper. The editor, Joseph Addison Turner, liked Joel, and took the boy to live on his plantation. Life on the plantation did much to shape the boy's future. Here were many good books to read. When Joel wanted to write, Turner helped him. When he was not busy, Joel could go to the slave cabins and listen to the Negroes tell stories.

In 1876 Harris began working on the Atlanta *Constitution*, and it was in this newspaper that his first Uncle Remus stories appeared. They were based on the stories he had heard as a child. The stories soon made Harris famous throughout much of the world.

One of the best-liked Uncle Remus stories is "The Wonderful Tar Baby." It tells of how "Br'er Fox" caught "Br'er Rabbit" one day with a sticky tar baby. At the end, "Br'er Rabbit" outsmarts the fox and gets away. Many books of Uncle Remus stories have been published. The titles of some of them are *Nights with Uncle Remus, Uncle Remus and Br'er Rabbit,* and *Mr. Rabbit at Home.* (See AMERICAN WRITERS.)

HARUN AL-RASHID (ha ROON ar ra SHEED) (764-809) In many stories of the *Arabian Nights* Harun al-Rashid is the hero. Aladdin and Sinbad and the many other heroes in the *Arabian Nights* were make-believe people. But Harun al-Rashid was a real person. He was the caliph, or prince, of Baghdad over 11½ centuries ago.

Baghdad is a city in the land now called Iraq. It has had a long, long history. Per-

haps the brightest time in all its history was the reign of Harun al-Rashid.

As the caliph of Baghdad, Harun al-Rashid ruled not only over the city but also over the eastern Moslem empire. The caliph did not do much about affairs of state. He left them mostly to his Grand Vizier, whose name was Yahya. Harun al-Rashid himself was more interested in making Baghdad a center of art and learning. He was a scholar and a poet, and he invited other scholars and poets to his court. He also invited musicians and storytellers. The stories about him in the *Arabian Nights* were made up by these storytellers.

In many of the stories Harun al-Rashid put on a disguise and went out at night among his people. He found out a great deal about what his subjects were doing and saying. Probably the stories are made up. But they are fun to read, and they help us remember the name of a famous ruler. (See ARABIAN NIGHTS; IRAQ.)

This famous caliph of Baghdad appears in the Arabian Nights.

Harvey discovered the true way in which blood circulates.

HARVEY, WILLIAM (1578-1657) Some 350 years ago William Harvey, a young Englishman, went to the University of Padua in Italy to study medicine. At that time doctors had strange notions about the work of the heart and the movement of blood through the body. They thought that the blood moved backward and forward like the ebb and flow of the tides. They thought that one kind of blood was made in the liver. The heart, they believed, made another kind of blood.

Another wrong idea was that arteries carried air to all parts of the body and that only veins carried blood. How blood could get from one side of the heart to the other was a mystery, since there is a thick wall between the two sides. The doctors of the time argued that there must be tiny holes in the wall for the blood to get through.

Harvey wondered about the truth of these ideas when they were taught to him. He decided to find out for himself.

When Harvey finished his work at the university, he returned to England and became a successful doctor. Before long he was appointed court physician to the king.

For many years Harvey studied the work of the heart and the flow of the blood by experimenting with animals. He studied his human patients carefully, too. Not till he was sure he had discovered the truth about the circulation of blood did he publish the results of his experiments.

The book he wrote, although it is now over 300 years old, is still worth reading. In it Harvey correctly describes the circulation of the blood. He was the very first person to do so.

Harvey's discoveries were not accepted at once by the other physicians of his time. Many people decided that he was crazy and would not trust him as their doctor. Before his death, however, most people knew that he was right. Today he is considered one of the greatest scientists of all time. (See BLOOD; HEART.)

HATS AND CAPS A whole book could easily be filled with pictures of kinds of hats and caps that have been worn by different groups of people at different times. There is room here for only a few.

People wear hats or caps for two main reasons. One is to protect the head from cold or sun or storm. The other is as a decoration to fit in with the fashions or customs of the time. In many countries more and more people are now going bareheaded even in cold weather. Hatmaking, however, is still an important kind of work. Many women and girls always have several hats, and many men and boys have more than one. Besides, hats and caps are a part of many uniforms. As a part of his uniform, for instance, every fireman, policeman, soldier, and sailor has a hat or cap.

Fur hats, of course, are worn usually in lands with cold winters. Fur is a good protection from cold. Broad-brimmed hats with tall crowns are most likely to be worn in regions where the sun is bright. The wide brim provides shade for the wearer's face. The air in the tall crown helps shut off the sun's heat.

Some kinds of hats are worn only on special occasions. A man, for instance, would never wear a silk top hat to a football game. But he might wear one to a wedding or some other formal occasion.

Hats play an important part in good manners. In some churches a woman is always expected to wear a hat. In some even men keep on their hats as a sign of respect. American men and boys take off their hats when they enter a house. On the street, if a man is wearing a hat, he tips it when he meets a lady he knows.

In some parts of the world hats change very little as the years go by. In others a

TYPES OF HATS

hat that is fashionable one year may be old-fashioned the next. Of course, the hats that go out of fashion fastest are the ones that are worn chiefly for decoration. (See CLOTHING; ETIQUETTE.)

HAWAII The Pacific is by far the world's biggest ocean. Scattered over it there are thousands of islands. These islands make stepping stones across the ocean. Boats and planes can stop at them. The Hawaiian Islands make the first stepping stone in traveling across the Pacific from the West Coast. The "step" to these islands is a giant one. They are over 2,000 miles out in the Pacific from the coast of California.

Hawaii is the largest of the Hawaiian Islands. The whole group of islands is called simply Hawaii, too. But the one big city in the islands is not on the island of Hawaii. The city is Honolulu. It is on the island of Oahu.

Stories of early voyages in the Pacific sometimes mention the Sandwich Islands. But there are no Sandwich Islands on maps now. This is the name by which the Hawaiian Islands were once known.

The Hawaiian Islands are famous for their climate, their volcanoes, and their pineapples. They are famous, too, because the naval base Pearl Harbor is there.

All the year round the climate of the islands is pleasant for bathing, boating, and surfboard riding. Tourists come by the

Tam-o'-shanter

Mexican Sombrero

Turbans

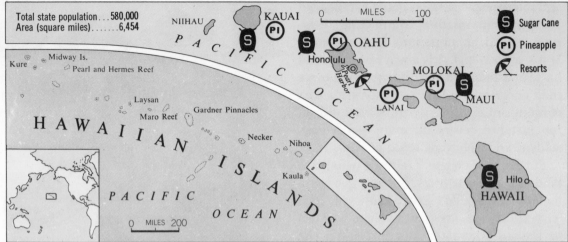

Total state population...580,000
Area (square miles)......6,454

S Sugar Cane
PI Pineapple
R Resorts

thousands every year to Honolulu. The city has beautiful hotels and beaches. Tourists are often greeted by Hawaiian girls wearing grass skirts and garlands of flowers. These garlands are called *leis* (LAYS).

The islands are partly the tops of volcanoes that rise up from the sea's floor. They have been built much larger by coral. The most famous volcano on the islands is Mauna Loa. One of its craters is almost three miles across.

Most of the world's pineapples come from Hawaii. Many people earn their living by raising them. Many others work in pineapple canning factories. Though pineapples are Hawaii's best-known crop, sugar is its most important one.

Many kinds of plants and animals have never reached these islands. There are, for instance, no native snakes or toads.

The native Hawaiians are brown-skinned people. There are several thousand on the islands. But many of the people now in Hawaii have come from other lands. There are many Japanese.

Before 1898 Hawaii was a country by itself. For most of its history it was ruled by a king or a queen. Its last royal ruler was Queen Liliuokalani. In 1898 its people asked that their country be made a part of the United States. It was made a territory by the United States Congress in 1900. In 1959 the wish of its people that Hawaii be made a state was granted. Hawaii became the 50th state of the United States. (See ISLANDS; PACIFIC OCEAN; PEARL HARBOR; SUGAR.)

HAWKING The two knights in the picture are going hunting. They do not have guns of any kind. In the days of knights, guns had not been invented. Instead of guns they have trained hawks. These hawks are trained to fly after small animals and kill them. The hawk is really both the knight's gun and his hunting dog.

Hunting with a hawk is called hawking. It is also called falconry. "Falcon" is another name for hawks of certain kinds.

Hawking is a very old sport. A picture made in Assyria 700 years before Christ

Pineapples are one of the major crops of Hawaii.

shows a falcon on the wrist of a hunter. All during the Middle Ages hawking was the favorite sport of kings and nobles. Hawking is still a sport today, but not many people take part in it.

A person interested in hawking has to train the hawk himself. But first he must get one. A good place to get one is from a nest of young hawks. These nests, however, are not easy to reach. Besides, hawks fight fiercely to protect their young.

A hawk must be trained just as a hunting dog is trained. The trainer should work with the hawk for several hours every day. Hawks are natural hunters. But it is not easy to teach them not to eat their prey. Even after weeks of training, a hawk may fly away when it is let loose, and never come back. It is almost sure to fly away if it is not well cared for.

To keep a hunting hawk, a person must have a high fence to protect the hawk from cats, and trees to protect it from the sun. He must feed it fresh meat such as freshly-killed pigeons or chickens.

A hunter who goes hawking wears a leather gauntlet on his wrist. His hawk's claws are very sharp. The hawk wears a hood to keep it from seeing an animal and flying after it before the hunter is ready. The hawk also wears leather bands called "jesses" on its legs. Above the jesses are two tiny bells. A leash is fastened to the jesses when the hawk is on its perch. The bells help the hunter keep track of the hawk.

Knights with Their Hawks

FRANZ JOSEPH HAYDN

HAYDN, FRANZ JOSEPH (1732-1809) The "Surprise Symphony" is one of the first symphonies boys and girls learn to know. It was written about 200 years ago by the great composer Haydn.

Haydn was born in a small town in Austria. His parents loved music, and Haydn as a boy heard good music in his home.

When he was only eight he became a choirboy in a great church in Vienna. He studied in the school of this church for several years. Then his voice changed and he could no longer be a choirboy.

For the next ten years Haydn's life was hard. He had almost no money, and he was often hungry and cold. But good fortune came at last. Haydn was made director of Austria's finest orchestra—the orchestra of Prince Esterhazy. He directed this orchestra for 30 years.

During these 30 years Haydn became famous all over Europe for his own music. He wrote more than 100 symphonies, more than 75 quartets, more than 50 sonatas, 3 oratorios, and much other music. He is called the father of the symphony and the founder of the string quartet. Not only the "Surprise Symphony" but many others of his compositions have lived on. Many are played by our great orchestras today. (See COMPOSERS; MUSIC; ORCHESTRA.)

FOODS FOR
GOOD HEALTH

HEALTH Good health is a great blessing. Everyone should do all he can to stay healthy. Being in good health means having both body and mind in good working order, free from disease and pain.

Good food, fresh air, exercise, good posture, plenty of rest, sunshine, plenty of water, comfortable clothing, cleanliness, and checkups with the doctor and dentist all help in keeping our body machines running as they should.

Food does many things for our bodies. It provides the materials for growing and for repairing worn-out parts. It gives us energy for work and play. It furnishes the "sparks" that keep all the parts of our bodies doing their work well. No one food gives us everything we need. We should eat foods of different kinds. Having enough to eat is not the same as having the right food.

Sleep is the best kind of rest. Growing children need more sleep than grownups. Children's bodies not only have to be repaired; they also have to grow. No one's body can grow bigger properly while he is working and playing and wearing it out.

Exercise makes muscles strong and helps us have good posture. It also makes blood rush through the body faster, carrying food and oxygen. Exercise in the fresh air and sunshine is especially good. Exercise should be fun, too. Healthy exercise that is fun helps keep us well mentally.

The water we drink helps wash away wastes formed inside our bodies. It also puts back the water we lose when we perspire. Our bodies are actually more than half water. We must drink enough to replace what we lose. Usually six glassfuls a day is about the right amount.

We feel better and look better when we are clean. A bath every day is a good rule for most of us. Brushing our teeth is an important part of keeping clean.

Clothing should be suited to the weather. On cold winter days clothes should keep in the body's heat. In hot summer weather clothes should let the body's heat escape.

Loose clothing is better than tight clothing because it allows the wearer to move about more easily and does not interfere with the circulation of the blood.

One should not wait to get sick or have a toothache before going to the doctor or dentist. A check-up is a kind of "stitch in time." Of course, if something is wrong, the doctor or dentist can do much toward making it right again.

It is a good idea to practice the rules of good health so well that they get to be habits. The earlier good health habits are formed, the better.

Even if a person has very good health habits, he will probably be sick once in a while. He may get an illness caused by disease germs. He can get these germs by being with sick people. He may get them through impure milk or water. Or they may be carried to him by insects or other animals. Germs in spoiled food may make him sick. Living in a damp, dark, dirty house may also help make him sick. And if he works in a factory, he may become sick from poisonous gases and harmful dust.

Today governments are doing a great deal to help keep people well. Governments are providing plenty of safe water, good sewage and garbage disposal, pleasant parks and playgrounds, and good housing. They have strong health departments ready to fight any disease that might spread.

Governments do more than try to keep people well. They run clinics and hospitals to treat sick people. They carry on experiments to learn more about diseases, too, for some diseases are still puzzles—their causes and cures are still unknown. Mental diseases are among the most puzzling.

It has benefited people and governments to work for good health. In the days of our cave-man ancestors, people lived an average of less than 20 years. Now the average is about 70 years. It has gone up 20 years just since the beginning of the present century! (See BODY, HUMAN; DISEASES; FOODS; SAFETY; SLEEP; VITAMINS; WATER SUPPLY.)

RULES FOR GOOD HEALTH

1. Good Food
2. Cleanliness
3. Plenty of Rest

The electrocardiograph shows how a person's heart is working.

HEART "I give you my heart" is another way of saying "I love you." "Stouthearted" is another word for "brave." "He has a good heart" means that he is kind. Once people thought that our feelings of love and bravery and kindness came from our hearts. Now we know that they do not. But we still talk as if they did.

A person's heart is about the size of his fist. It is about the same shape and weighs less than a pound. A real heart does not look much like the hearts on valentines.

We do not feel with our hearts, but they are very important. Blood must be kept moving in our bodies every minute of our lives. It must carry food and oxygen to all parts of the body and take away waste materials. The blood travels through blood vessels of three kinds: arteries, veins, and capillaries. The heart keeps the blood moving.

The heart is really two pumps in one. One half of the heart makes blood flow to the lungs and back again. The other half sends the blood over the rest of the body.

Each half of the heart has two rooms: an auricle and a ventricle. The auricle on the *left* side of the heart receives blood that has just come from the lungs. The *left* auricle sends the blood into the *left* ventricle. The left ventricle then squeezes the blood into a big artery called the aorta. The aorta has branches going all over the body.

The blood flows from them into tiny capillaries. From the capillaries it flows into veins. They carry it to the *right* auricle. From there it goes to the *right* ventricle. The right ventricle sends it through arteries to the lungs. It flows through the capillaries in the lungs, then into veins and back to the heart to start over again.

There are valves in the heart. They are doors that keep the blood from flowing the wrong way.

The walls of the heart are mostly muscle. The muscles of the heart never get a rest as the muscles in our arms and legs do. The pump must keep working. Every time the heart muscles contract and force the blood out into the arteries we say there is a heartbeat. The surge of blood at each heartbeat can be felt in the wrist. Counting these surges is called taking the pulse. The opening and closing of the valves in the heart make a noise that a doctor can hear with his stethoscope. Our hearts beat faster at some times than at others. But they always beat many times a minute—sometimes more than 100. Normally children's hearts beat from 80 to 100 times per minute.

Many other animals have hearts. But of all animals with hearts, only birds and mammals have hearts with four rooms like ours. (See BLOOD; BODY, HUMAN; BREATHING; HARVEY, WILLIAM.)

Our sun's surface temperature is about 11,000°F.

HEAT In ancient times people thought that heat was a material just as air is. They called it "caloric." When something got warm, they said, caloric flowed into it. When something cooled off, caloric flowed out of it. It did not bother them that they could not see caloric. They could not see air either.

Now we know that heat is not a material. It does not take up any space. It does not weigh anything. It is a form of energy instead. Saying that heat is a form of energy means that it can be used to do work. When we see an automobile speeding down a road, we can be sure that it is being driven by the heat of burning gasoline.

There are many ways of producing heat. Fire, friction, and electricity are three of them. All of our ways of producing heat, however, would not keep the earth warm enough for us to live on it if it were not for the sun. In the sun changes are going on that keep it so hot that we can hardly imagine how very hot it is. It has given the earth heat for millions of years. It will keep on giving the earth heat for millions of years to come.

Heat travels much better through some materials than through others. It travels easily through metals. We say that they are good conductors of heat. Wool, asbestos, and still air are three of the many poor conductors of heat. We use poor conductors to shut heat in or to shut it out.

Heat can also travel without the use of any material conductor. The sun's heat reaches us across almost empty space in the form of rays which the sun sends out.

Most substances expand, or get bigger, when they are heated. Engineers must allow room for expansion when they build concrete roads and steel bridges.

Heat brings about many other changes in materials. Heating some solid substances makes them melt. Heating liquids makes them change to a vapor, or gas. In many foods heat brings about changes which make the foods pleasanter to eat.

Cold means absence of heat. We can cool something only by making heat travel out of it. In a refrigerator we do not put cold into the food. We take heat out.

Knowing how heat can be produced, how it travels, and what kinds of changes it brings about is important to all of us. (See ELECTRICITY; ENERGY; ENGINES, HEAT; FIRE; FRICTION; FUELS; HEATING AND VENTILATION; SUN.)

Temperatures of Four Bright Stars

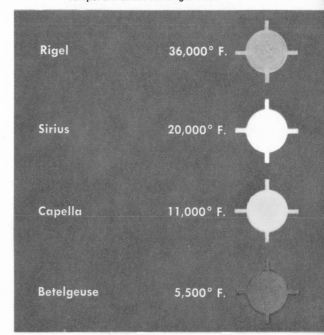

Rigel	36,000° F.
Sirius	20,000° F.
Capella	11,000° F.
Betelgeuse	5,500° F.

HEATING AND VENTILATION Many people live in parts of the world with cold winters. They are able to do so partly because they have learned to make warm clothing and partly because they have learned to heat their buildings. Most of the heating is done with fire.

The idea of heating with fire is not new. Thousands of years ago the cave men were using fire for heating.

Probably the earliest way of heating a room was simply to build a fire in the middle of the room. Since the earliest floors were earth or rock, fires could be built on them safely.

The Romans worked out a way of heating all the rooms in their houses with one fire. The fire was built in a room called the atrium. "Atrium" means "black room." It got its name from the soot that coated its walls. From this room hot air was carried through pipes to the rest of the house.

Heating all the rooms of a building from one source of heat is called central heating. After the days of the Romans, the idea of central heating was given up for 1,500 years. People went back to the idea of a fire in each room. But they found better ways of heating than simply having a bonfire on the floor.

Moving the fire from the center to one side of the room was a start toward a fireplace. At first there was only a hole in the roof above the fire to let out the smoke. But in time someone found a way of building a kind of hood to guide the smoke to the opening. At last real chimneys were built, and fireplaces came to look much as they do now. Many of the fireplaces in medieval castles were so large that they burned logs too big for one man to carry.

The first stoves were built at about the end of the Middle Ages. The ancient Egyptians used metal pans called braziers for carrying hot coals from place to place. But the idea of shutting fire up in stoves was slow in coming. Once people had the idea, stoves of many kinds were invented. Benjamin Franklin made a stove by putting an iron jacket around a fireplace grate. For years Franklin stoves were popular throughout the United States.

In a central heating system, hot air, hot water, or steam is sent from a furnace through pipes into the rooms of a building. A fire in a furnace heats the air or the water in hot air and hot water furnaces. In steam heating systems it heats water so hot that it turns to steam. Coal or oil or gas may be burned in the furnace.

The simplest hot air and hot water furnaces work because air and water are lighter when they are hot than when they are cold. Hot air and hot water are constantly being pushed up from the furnace by cooler air and water. In many furnaces there are fans or pumps to help push the air or water through the pipes.

In a steam heating system steam forces itself through the pipes because steam takes up much more space than the water it comes from. Steam heats a building very well, because it is very hot as it leaves the boiler of a furnace. It also gives off a great deal of heat as it changes back to water. A vapor pressure system is much like a system that uses steam, but the "steam" is not as hot.

In most hot air systems the hot air enters a room through an opening called a register. Cold air goes back to the furnace through another register. Steam, hot water, and the vapor in a vapor pressure system as a rule travel through radiators in each room of a building. They may travel instead through pipes that are hidden in the floors or walls of each room. Heating in this way is called radiant heating.

Electric heaters can heat rooms, and panels carrying electric wiring may be built into walls. Heating with such panels is another type of radiant heating.

Experiments are now being carried on with sun, or solar, heating. The house pictured is heated by a solar heating system. There are other ways of using the sun to heat a house, too. But a house with a solar heating system needs another heating system for cold, cloudy days.

The air inside an Eskimo igloo may be very warm. The entrance to the igloo is through a long tunnel which protects the doorway from wind. The igloo may be lined with skins. The layer of air between the skins and the snow helps shut heat in. In fact, heat is shut in so well that small oil lamps give off all the heat needed. But not many people would be willing to trade our ways of heating for the simple Eskimo way. For the Eskimos practically live inside a stove. There is no way for the gas from the oil lamps to escape or for fresh air to come in. We think that it is just as important to keep the air in a room fresh and odorless as it is to keep it warm. Changing the air in a room is called ventilation.

People used to believe that stale air was likely to give people headaches chiefly because much of the oxygen had been used up and carbon dioxide had been formed in its place. Now scientists have found out that the moisture people give off as they breathe helps make air stale. They have found out, too, that even if no fresh air is brought into a room, it helps to make the air in the room move.

One way of ventilating a room is simply to open windows in it. Fans may be used to blow in fresh air and blow out stale air. Today heating systems and ventilating systems are often combined. When hot air is used, for instance, air may be brought in from outdoors to be heated. In some ventilating systems the air is washed. In some it passes through filters. These ways of ventilating are air conditioning systems. Many people think of air conditioning as being for hot weather only. But keeping the air in a building free from dust and odors is good in cold weather, too. With good heating and ventilation we can have pleasant summer weather inside our houses all winter long. (See AIR CONDITIONING; FIRE; FUELS.)

Wood Fire

Fireplace

Franklin Stove

Furnace

Electric Room Heater

Steam Radiator

Solar Heating

Collector

Hot Air

To Tank

To Roof Collector

Storage Tank

Water moving through pipes in the big heat collectors is heated by the sun. The heated water goes to a storage tank. It is used to warm air which is forced to all the rooms in the house.

Piasecki Helicopter

HELICOPTER A helicopter can fly forward just as an airplane does. But it can do many things an airplane cannot do. It can fly straight up or straight down. It can fly backwards or sideways. It can hover almost motionless over one spot. It can take off or land on a very small field. A helicopter does not need runways.

Helicopters are easy to tell from airplanes. Helicopters do not have wings. Above them they have sets of blades that whirl around. Each blade acts much like a wing. Each set of blades is called a rotor. A helicopter may have just one main rotor. If it does, it also has a little rotor on the tail. If it has more than one main rotor, it does not need a rotor on its tail. Because of their rotors helicopters are sometimes called "whirly birds."

The air moving over the whirling blades of the main rotor gives the "lift" needed to make a helicopter fly. The pilot can tilt the rotor blades to make the helicopter go in any direction or make it hover. The tail

rotor is a kind of rudder. Of course, an engine turns the rotors.

The idea of a helicopter is not new. The Italian genius Leonardo da Vinci planned one more than 400 years ago. He even built models that sometimes worked. More models were made later. But useful helicopters are much newer than airplanes. In the United States Igor Sikorsky, a famous aircraft designer, made the first successful helicopter flight in 1939.

Helicopters are helpful in many ways. Here are a few of the jobs they can do:

Carry mail from airports to city post offices.

Help policemen guide holiday traffic on crowded roads.

Carry passengers for short flights between neighboring airports.

Sikorsky Helicopter

Help forest rangers patrol forests.

Assist in cattle roundups.

Help farmers spray their fields.

Rescue people trapped on ice fields or high on mountaintops.

Carry troops behind enemy lines and rescue trapped and wounded soldiers during time of war.

Helicopters are not easy to fly. It takes even a good airplane pilot many hours of practice to learn to manage a helicopter well. And helicopters, although useful, will never take the place of airplanes for carrying passengers and cargoes long distances. Although the fastest can travel about 150 miles an hour, airplanes can go much faster than that. (See AIRPLANES.)

S-55 Sikorsky Helicopter

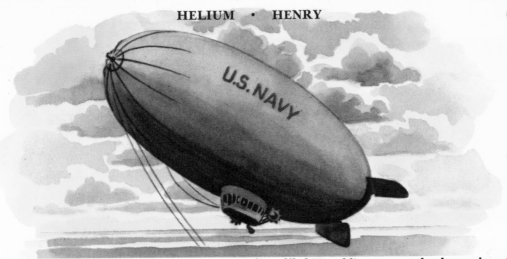

Helium-filled Navy blimps are used to hunt submarines.

HELIUM Blimps like the one in the picture are often filled with helium. Helium is a very light gas. Although not as light as the gas hydrogen, it is much better for blimps and balloons for one reason. It will not burn.

The name of this gas comes from the Greek word for sun. In 1868 scientists discovered helium in the sun. Nearly 30 years later they discovered it on the earth.

Helium is found in natural gas. Practically all the helium in the world is produced in the United States. The most important production plant is in Texas.

Although helium is rather scarce here on the earth, there is a great deal of it in the universe. All the billions of stars are made up mostly of helium and hydrogen. (See BALLOONS; HYDROGEN.)

HENRY, PATRICK (1736-1799) Visitors to Richmond, Va., are often taken to see the church where Patrick Henry worshiped and to places where he made some of his famous speeches. Richmond is proud of Patrick Henry because he was a great orator and a great patriot.

In one of his most famous speeches, Henry shouted, "But as for me, give me liberty or give me death." This speech was made nearly 200 years ago, in the days of the 13 colonies. Patrick Henry was urging the colonies to fight for freedom from England's rule. Not long afterward the colonies fought the Revolutionary War and became a free country.

Patrick Henry was born in Virginia. As a boy he was not interested in school. He went to work as soon as he was old enough. First he tried keeping a store but was not a success. Next he tried being a farmer but failed at this, too. Then he decided to study law. He liked it so much that he became a lawyer in a very short time.

From then on he took a great interest in government. His speeches helped bring about the Revolution. Afterward he was the governor of Virginia for several terms. He served many terms in the Virginia legislature, too. He can be thanked for some good changes in the constitution of the new country he had helped found. Patrick Henry is on every list of American patriots. (See PATRIOTS.)

PATRICK HENRY

Giraffes are large herbivorous animals.

HERBIVOROUS ANIMALS Animals that eat nothing but plants are called herbivorous animals. All animals get their food from plants. But some get it by eating animals that eat plants. The herbivorous animals eat the plants themselves.

In every place where there are any animals at all there must be some plant eaters. If there weren't, there would be no food for the meat eaters.

There are thousands and thousands of kinds of herbivorous animals. Some are small, some are medium-sized, and some are large. Tree hoppers and butterflies and water fleas are herbivorous. So are rabbits and squirrels and many fishes. Horses, cows, camels, giraffes, and zebras are herbivorous, too. There are a great many others besides.

Some animals are herbivorous for only a part of their lives. Frogs and toads eat plants when they are tadpoles. They are meat eaters after they grow up.

Plant eaters have one big advantage over meat eaters. Their food cannot run away from them. They do not have to be such active animals. On the other hand, most plant food is harder to digest than meat. Besides, a plant eater must eat a great deal of food to get all the nourishment it has to

Buffalo Tree Hopper

Baby cottontail rabbits start hopping around and nibbling when only two weeks old.

have. A horse out on pasture has to eat grass most of the day, while a cat can eat enough meat in a few minutes to last it for hours. (See CARNIVOROUS ANIMALS; HOOFED ANIMALS; OMNIVOROUS ANIMALS.)

HERBS (URBS) Trees have woody stems. So do bushes, or shrubs. But there are many green plants that do not have any wood in their stems. These plants are called herbs.

Herbs grow in different ways. Some, like dandelions, are low-growing; they never get far above the ground. Others, like sunflowers, grow to be several feet tall. Still others are vines.

The stems of herbs have a great deal of water in them. The water in them makes them firm and usually able to stand erect. Because herb stems have so much water in them, they freeze when cold weather comes. But, although the stems may die

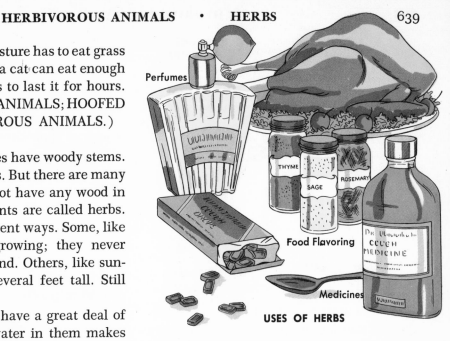

Perfumes

THYME

SAGE ROSEMARY

Food Flavoring

COUGH MEDICINE

Medicines

USES OF HERBS

down to the ground in the winter, some herbs are able to live on year after year. They may live on underground and send up new stems and leaves in the spring. Some of these herbs have underground stems that stay alive during cold weather; some have big roots; some have bulbs.

The word "herb" has another meaning to many people. It means plants used to flavor other foods. The pictures below show some herbs of this kind. Whole gardens of herbs like these used to be common. Perfumes, too, are sometimes made from the herbs in herb gardens.

"Herb" has still another meaning. It may mean a plant from which medicine is made. There used to be many herb doctors. We still get some medicines from herbs. (See COOKING; SHRUBS; TREES; VINES.)

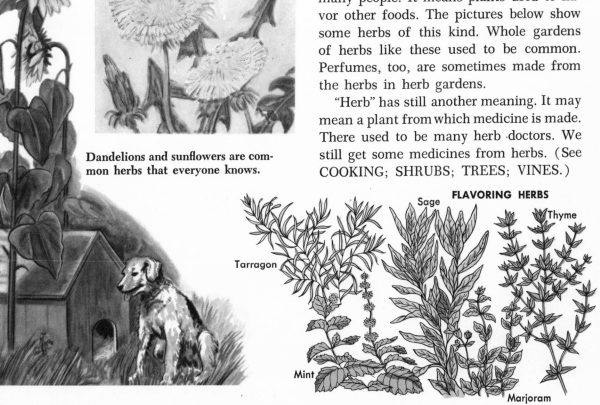

Dandelions and sunflowers are common herbs that everyone knows.

FLAVORING HERBS

Sage

Thyme

Tarragon

Mint

Marjoram

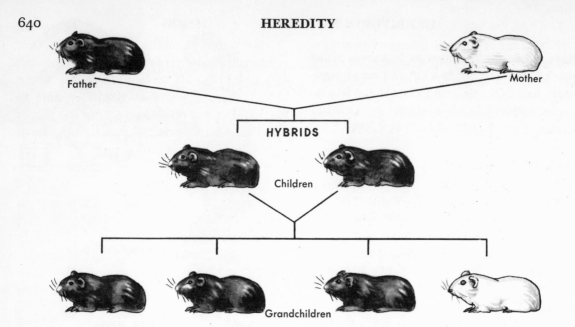

Father

Mother

HYBRIDS

Children

Grandchildren

HEREDITY No one expects to raise a rosebush by planting a hollyhock seed. No one expects a bluebird's eggs to hatch into peacocks. But why is it that young plants and animals are always much like the plants and animals that produced them? The answer is that every living thing inherits, or gets from its ancestors, a great deal. It may inherit ways of doing things as well as such things as size and shape and color. An oriole, for example, does not have to be taught how to build a wonderful hanging nest

Heredity is another name for inheriting. Scientists know now that living things inherit their characteristics because of very, very tiny particles called genes. They are a part of the cells all living things are made of. An apple tree raised from a branch of another apple tree will be very, very much like the tree it came from if it has the same chance to grow. Its genes are just like those in the parent tree. In the same way a sponge that comes from a bit broken off from a full-grown sponge will be almost exactly like its parent. Its genes are the same.

Most plants and animals, however, have two parents. They get some of their genes from one of these parents and some from the other. The seed from a hollyhock with single flowers would certainly not produce a rose, but it might produce a plant with double flowers. A black mother cat might well have a white kitten.

Scientists who study heredity have done much experimenting with crossing plants and animals that are quite different in certain ways. The man who started scientists to experimenting with heredity was an Austrian monk, Gregor Mendel. He found out a great deal about heredity by experimenting with the plants in the monastery garden. He worked out some laws about heredity that are called Mendel's laws.

The chart above shows what to expect when a rough-haired white guinea pig is mated with a smooth-haired black guinea pig. All the guinea pigs they produce are black and rough-haired. They get genes for a smooth black coat from one parent and genes for a rough white coat from the other. But the genes for roughness and for blackness have more effect than have those for smoothness and whiteness. These guinea pigs, however, pass on the genes for smoothness and whiteness to some of their children. Some of the third generation may be more like one of their grandparents than they are like their parents.

If a plant or animal inherits two different genes for some characteristic, one may not have any more effect than the other. If a red cow and a white bull are mated, the calves are likely to be roan—halfway between red and white.

Knowing something about heredity has helped scientists develop plants and animals that suit our purposes better than those we had before. It has helped, for instance, to develop hybrid corn, which has produced much bigger yields and much better corn than any earlier corn.

Once in a while a plant or animal may show a decided change—a change that cannot be explained by studying the ancestors of the plant or animal. A plant raised from the seed of a vine, for instance, may be a dwarf bush instead. And it may pass on dwarfness to the plants raised from its seeds. New plants and animals that show such sudden changes are called sports, or mutants. Scientists explain them by saying that something happened to bring about a change in the genes.

Not many sports, or mutants, are changed in desirable ways. But some are. If scientists knew how to bring about changes in genes, they might be able to speed up the work of improving the plants and animals we raise. They are doing much experimenting. For one thing, they are trying the use of atomic energy to bring about changes in genes.

Heredity is as important for people as for other living things. Scientists do not know as much about it in people as in many other living things because they do not have a chance to experiment. But they are finding out more and more about what can be inherited and what cannot be.

Scientists know, for instance, that a skilful carpenter cannot pass on to his children his skill. The children have to learn that for themselves if they, too, want to become carpenters. But the carpenter's children may inherit well-built hands that will make learning to use tools easy. The child of an astronomy professor cannot inherit what his father knows about the stars, but he can inherit a good mind that will let him learn about the stars. A child cannot inherit tuberculosis, but he can inherit a tendency to get the disease if germs enter his body.

There is still a great deal about heredity that no one understands. And today more scientists than ever before are trying to solve some of its puzzles. (See CELL; DWARFS; GIANTS; GOLDFISH; GRAFTING; HYBRIDS; MENDEL, GREGOR.)

The loganberry is a mutant believed to have come from a wild blackberry.

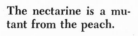

The nectarine is a mutant from the peach.

HIBERNATION Most living things have a way of escaping cold weather and lack of food. Plants drop their leaves and rest. Many birds, a few insects, and some other animals migrate. People put on warmer clothes, start a fire in the furnace, and either eat food they have stored up or buy it from the grocery store. Some animals hibernate. Hibernation is sometimes called "winter sleep."

Scientists believe that most animals that hibernate do so because of falling temperatures. They point out that most hibernators are cold-blooded. When the surrounding temperature falls, theirs fall also. Heat is necessary for life activities to go on. So cold-blooded animals almost stop living when winter comes.

Amphibians burrow in the mud, among sticks and stones, and in rotting tree trunks. If one were to dig up a hibernating frog, it would appear to be dead. There would be no air in its lungs, and its heartbeat would be too slow to be detected. A hibernating frog remains in this half-alive state until spring. Among the other cold-blooded animals that hibernate are many butterflies and other insects, land snails, and reptiles.

Some mammals hibernate, too. Temperature probably is not the reason for mammal hibernation, since mammals are warm-blooded. Scientists believe that mammals

Bear Hibernating in Cave

Mouse Finding Shelter

Top of Beaver Lodge
Above Water

Fish Keeping Active While Turtles and Frogs Sleep in Mud

hibernate because of lack of food. These animals store up fat in the summer and then curl up in a burrow or den for the winter. Some even hide food or take it into the den with them. In the close space the heat from their bodies keeps the animals warm enough. All living activities are greatly slowed. The animals use up the stored fat little by little. Bears in cold regions may enter their dens sleek and fat in the fall and come out thin and lean in the spring.

Among the other mammals that hibernate are woodchucks, skunks, ground squirrels, some tree squirrels, and bats. (See AMPHIBIANS; BEARS; REPTILES; SLEEP; TOADS AND FROGS.)

HIMALAYAS In the whole world there are only five mountains more than five miles high. They are all in the Himalayas. Mt. Everest is the highest of them. It measures just over 29,000 ft.

Until 1953 no one had ever been able to climb Mt. Everest although many had tried. On May 29 of that year Edmund Hillary of New Zealand and Tensing Norkay of Nepal reached the top.

Mt. Kanchenjunga is the most beautiful of the five great peaks. It is about 1,000 feet lower than Everest. A British expedition led by Charles Evans climbed to six feet from the top of this mountain in 1955. To please the natives they did not climb the last few feet.

The Himalayas are in central Asia. They form a great wall between Tibet and India. For hundreds of miles this wall cannot be crossed on land. Many of the peaks are more than three miles high. During World War II the Himalayas were called "the Hump." Planes flew over the Hump to carry supplies from India to China.

Some mountains are playgrounds. But not the Himalayas. The southern slopes are very rainy, and dense forests grow on them. The northern slopes are bleak and bare. In winter the weather is bitterly cold. "Himalaya" means "home of snow."

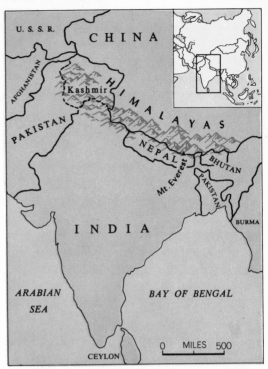

Mt. Everest is located in the Himalayas.

In a story about the Himalayas called *Lost Horizon*, there was a valley named Shangri-La. It was a beautiful valley in the midst of the bleak, snow-covered mountains. Shangri-La has now come to mean a lovely place hidden away in some distant part of the world.

The Himalayas are young mountains. They are not many million years old. They were pushed up at the same time that the Alps were made. They are much younger than the Rockies and the Andes and much, much younger than the Appalachians. (See ALPS; ANDES; APPALACHIANS; EXPLORERS; MOUNTAINS, ROCKY MOUNTAINS; TIBET.)

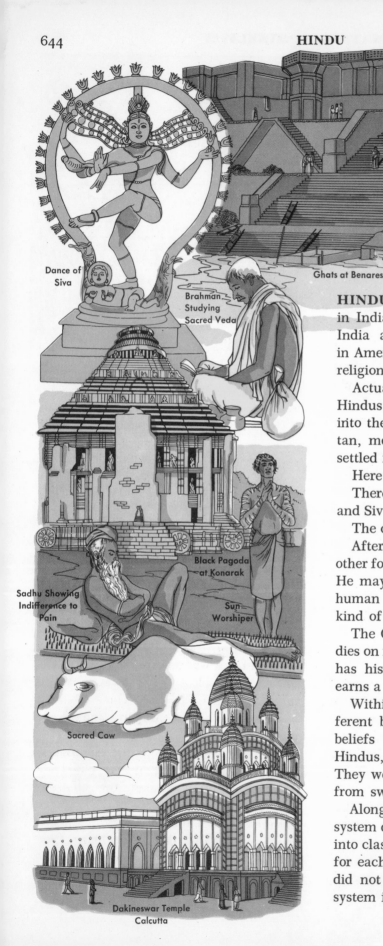

Dance of Siva

Brahman Studying Sacred Veda

Ghats at Benares

Yogi Practicing Physical Control

Black Pagoda at Konarak

Sun Worshiper

Sadhu Showing Indifference to Pain

Sacred Cow

Dakineswar Temple Calcutta

HINDU Many people think that everyone in India is a Hindu. Calling everyone in India a Hindu is like calling everyone in America a Christian. For Hinduism is a religion just as Christianity is.

Actually most of the people of India *are* Hindus. For when the old India was divided into the two countries of India and Pakistan, most Indians who were not Hindus settled in Pakistan.

Here are some of the Hindu beliefs:

There are many gods. Brahma, Vishnu, and Siva are the greatest.

The cow is sacred. It must not be killed.

After death everyone is reborn in another form. He may be reborn as an animal. He may be reborn higher in the scale of human beings. Everything depends on the kind of life he has led.

The Ganges River is sacred. If a Hindu dies on its banks or if he dies elsewhere but has his ashes thrown into the river, he earns a rest from being reborn.

Within the Hindu religion there are different beliefs, just as there are different beliefs in the Christian religion. Some Hindus, for instance, call all life sacred. They wear cloths over their faces to keep from swallowing tiny insects.

Along with the Hindu religion a caste system developed. All Hindus were divided into classes called castes. Rules were made for each caste. A person "lost caste" if he did not obey these rules. Now the caste system is breaking down.

The hide of a hippopotamus is very thick and heavy — it may weigh 500 lbs.

In Hindu temples there are many images of the Hindu gods. Some of them have several arms. These arms show that the gods have many powers. (See INDIA; RELIGIONS OF THE WORLD.)

HIPPOPOTAMUS The hippopotamus is found wild only in Africa, but almost every zoo has at least one. It stands captivity well. Many baby hippopotamuses have been born in captivity.

"Hippopotamus" comes from Greek words meaning "river horse." Half of the name is a good one, for the hippopotamus spends much time in streams. But a hippopotamus is not much like a horse. It is a much closer relative of the pig.

The hippopotamus is bigger than any land animal except the elephant. A big hippopotamus may weigh four tons. With its little beady eyes, tiny ears, and enormous mouth it is not a beautiful animal.

This big animal often lies with only its flat face above water. It can then see, hear,

and breathe, and still be well hidden by the muddy water of the river. It can also close its nose and stay under water for a few minutes at a time.

The hippopotamus is a plant eater. It needs several bushels of food a day. In its big mouth it has some tusks which help it dig up plants by their roots.

When a hippopotamus is excited its perspiration is red. The animal seems to be, but is not really, sweating blood.

The closest relative of the hippopotamus is the pig.

HISTORY History is the story of how today came to be. It is the story of what people all through the ages have thought and done and of what has happened to them.

The story of people begins a very long time ago. Perhaps there have been people on the earth for a million years. We do not know much about the early part of the story. For hundreds of thousands of years our ancestors struggled upward. But they did not make any record of their struggles. They couldn't. They did not know how to write.

The history of people before anyone could write sometimes isn't called history at all. Some people feel that the word "history" should only be used for recorded history.

Recorded history is a small chapter in the whole story. For people have been able to write for only about the past 5,000 years. All that we know about their story for the centuries upon centuries before that comes from things they made and left behind.

Recorded history is divided into three parts—ancient, medieval, and modern history. Ancient history tells the story of the world from about 3,000 B.C. to the fall of Rome about 1,500 years ago. Medieval history tells the story of the next 1,000 years. This period of time is called the Middle Ages. Modern history begins not long after the New World was discovered.

The history of different parts of the world varies greatly. The people of the Near East, for instance, could write long before any of the people of Europe could do so. At the time the people of Europe were building great cathedrals, the natives of middle Africa were building nothing bigger or more lasting than grass huts.

Some happenings have been so important as to stand out above the millions of others. These pages tell a picture story of a few of those important happenings. They tell a little of what was going on in other parts of the world at the same time.

500,000 B.C.

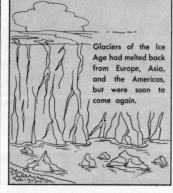

Glaciers of the Ice Age had melted back from Europe, Asia, and the Americas, but were soon to come again.

There was apparently no human life in the Western Hemisphere until many thousands of years later.

Men of the Old Stone Age lived in caves in Europe, Africa, and Asia. They had learned to use fire.

20,000 B.C.

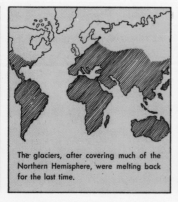

The glaciers, after covering much of the Northern Hemisphere, were melting back for the last time.

Cave men in southern Europe painted and carved with artistic skill. We can still see some of their paintings.

Ancestors of the Indians were moving from Asia into North America. They had fire and used stone tools.

6000 B.C.

In the Near East man had settled in the rich valleys and had learned how to domesticate plants and animals.

In Europe man was a simple food gatherer, but he had domesticated the dog.

The Indians were spreading southward throughout both North and South America.

3100 B.C.

Egypt was a united kingdom under a ruling family. The capital was at Memphis on the Nile River.

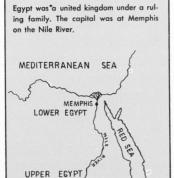

MEDITERRANEAN SEA

MEMPHIS
LOWER EGYPT

RED SEA

NILE RIVER

UPPER EGYPT

In Mesopotamia people were writing. They had wheeled vehicles and were making tools out of copper.

The Chinese had domesticated plants and animals. They had not yet learned to write.

2600 B.C.

The Egyptians built the Great Pyramid as a tomb for King Khufu. They used huge blocks of stone.

In Mesopotamian cities the people were building great temples out of bricks much like those of today. They had no stone.

Stone Age Lake Dwellers lived along the edges of lakes in Switzerland and in the northern part of Italy.

1750 B.C.

Hammurabi, famous ruler of Babylonia in Mesopotamia, gave a code of laws to his people.

Invaders were ruining a great civilization in the Indus Valley that had lasted some 600 years.

A shepherd people was moving down from the north into the Greek peninsula and settling there.

1500 B.C.

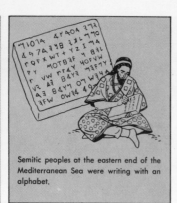

Semitic peoples at the eastern end of the Mediterranean Sea were writing with an alphabet.

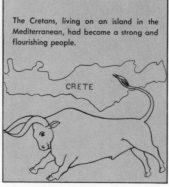

The Cretans, living on an island in the Mediterranean, had become a strong and flourishing people.

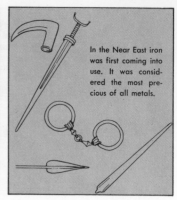

In the Near East iron was first coming into use. It was considered the most precious of all metals.

1400 B.C.

Crete fell before raiding parties of the Greeks. The Minoan civilization of the Cretans soon began to decline.

Under Thutmose III and other warrior pharaohs, Egypt had begun conquering other peoples and building an empire.

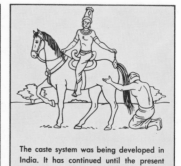

The caste system was being developed in India. It has continued until the present day, but is now disappearing.

1275 B.C.

The Hebrews, led by Moses, crossed the Red Sea into the Sinai peninsula and escaped from captivity in Egypt.

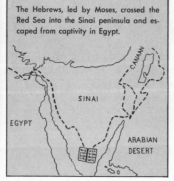

The Hittites, had built a powerful empire in Asia Minor. Their strength was due partly to rich stores of iron ore.

Along the Hwang Ho the Chinese had advanced far in farming. They had learned to write and keep records.

1200 B.C.

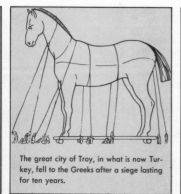

The great city of Troy, in what is now Turkey, fell to the Greeks after a siege lasting for ten years.

The Philistines were settling on the coast of the land that still carries their name — Palestine.

A Stone Age people whose ancestors had built the mysterious Stonehenge monument lived on the British Isles.

1002 B.C.

David became the second king of Israel. The Hebrews had conquered part of Palestine and had settled there.

The Greeks were setting up city-states. Among them were Sparta, Athens, Thebes, and Corinth.

GREECE

BLACK SEA

IONIAN SEA

AEGEAN SEA

MEDITERRANEAN SEA

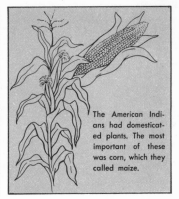

The American Indians had domesticated plants. The most important of these was corn, which they called maize.

959 B.C.

King Solomon began to build the great temple at Jerusalem that served as the holy center of Judaism for 1,000 years.

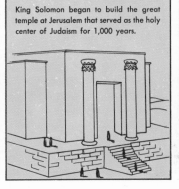

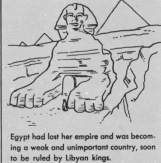

Egypt had lost her empire and was becoming a weak and unimportant country, soon to be ruled by Libyan kings.

Phoenicians sailed the Mediterranean. They were going all the way to the British Isles to get tin.

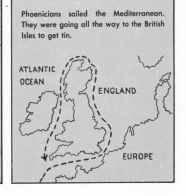

ATLANTIC OCEAN

ENGLAND

EUROPE

846 B.C.

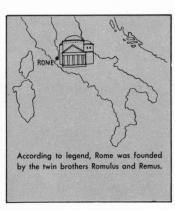

Carthage was founded on the northern coast of Africa by the Phoenicians for use as a trading post.

The blind Greek poet Homer was telling the stories that were later written down as the *Iliad* and the *Odyssey*.

Ancestors of the Eskimos had moved into the Arctic and were working out a way of life there.

753 B.C.

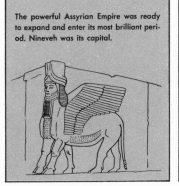

ROME

According to legend, Rome was founded by the twin brothers Romulus and Remus.

The powerful Assyrian Empire was ready to expand and enter its most brilliant period. Nineveh was its capital.

The Greeks were writing with the alphabet brought to them from the Near East by the seafaring Phoenicians.

594 B.C.

Solon, a great lawmaker and general, made new laws for the Greek city-state of Athens.

The civilization of the Etruscans flourished on the Italian peninsula. Etruscan kings ruled early Rome.

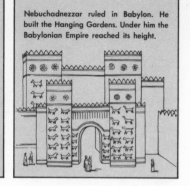

Nebuchadnezzar ruled in Babylon. He built the Hanging Gardens. Under him the Babylonian Empire reached its height.

525 B.C.

Persia conquered Egypt. She now controlled all the land at the eastern end of the Mediterranean Sea.

Greek merchants had brought the alphabet to the Italian peninsula.

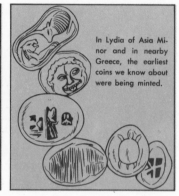

In Lydia of Asia Minor and in nearby Greece, the earliest coins we know about were being minted.

490 B.C.

At the battle of Marathon the Greek forces defeated the powerful army of the Persians and kept them from overrunning Europe.

Rome had overthrown its Etruscan rulers and had developed its own republican form of government.

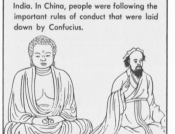

Buddha had founded a new religion in India. In China, people were following the important rules of conduct that were laid down by Confucius.

323 B.C.

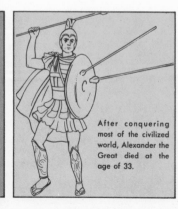

After conquering most of the civilized world, Alexander the Great died at the age of 33.

Rome, growing in strength, was fighting her neighbors for more territory throughout the Italian peninsula.

Carthage had become one of the world's great cities, and a powerful rival of Rome.

202 B.C.

Carthage's great general, Hannibal, led a huge army against the Romans and was defeated.

Buddhism, the religion founded by Buddha, had made many converts in India and was spreading throughout other lands in Asia.

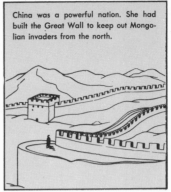

China was a powerful nation. She had built the Great Wall to keep out Mongolian invaders from the north.

146 B.C.

Roman forces destroyed Carthage. Rome was now without a rival in the western part of the Mediterranean.

Greece was a province of Rome. Her culture and thought had greatly influenced Roman thought, art, architecture, and literature.

In Egypt, under the Greek Ptolemies, Alexandria had become one of the greatest cities in the world.

4 B.C.

Jesus Christ was born in Bethlehem, which was a small city in the Roman province of Judea.

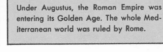

Under Augustus, the Roman Empire was entering its Golden Age. The whole Mediterranean world was ruled by Rome.

Britain had been invaded by Julius Caesar and was soon to become a Roman province.

105

In China the invention of paper was reported to the emperor. The invention paved the way for the spread of literature.

St. Paul had established the first Christian church. The Christian faith was spreading through the Roman Empire.

The Roman cities of Pompeii and Herculaneum lay buried under the ashes of the eruption of Vesuvius in A.D. 79.

313

Christianity was recognized as a legal religion in the Roman Empire by the Emperor Constantine.

In India Buddhism was giving way to Hinduism. India was about to enter a Golden Age of Hindu thought and rule.

The Japanese had a highly developed civilization. They had learned the art of writing from China.

410

Rome was looted by Visigoths led by Alaric. The Visigoths were Germanic tribesmen from the north.

In 330 the capital of the Roman Empire was moved from Rome to Constantinople, in what is now Turkey.

The Huns had advanced westward from the Gobi Desert into central Europe, burning and plundering as they came.

476

The city of Rome fell to German tribes from the north, and the Middle Ages of Europe began.

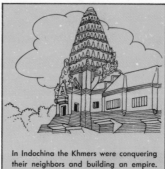
In Indochina the Khmers were conquering their neighbors and building an empire. Their capital was Angkor.

The Mayan Indians were building a great empire and culture in Central America and in Mexico.

622

Mohammed, an Arab, founded a new religion in Arabia. It spread quickly throughout the Near East.

Rome was the ruling center of the Christian world. The head of the Church was the bishop of Rome, who was called the pope.

The Angles, Saxons, and Jutes, Germanic tribes, had invaded Britain and were dominating it.

800

The pope crowned Charlemagne Emperor of the West. This was done in Rome on Christmas Day.

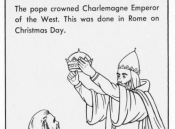

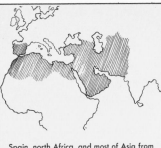

Spain, north Africa, and most of Asia from India westward were in the hands of the Mohammedans.

The Vikings, or Northmen, were plundering and terrorizing the towns along the northern coast of Europe.

899

Alfred the Great of England died. He had built up the navy and defeated Danish invaders. The Danes, however, still ruled part of Britain.

Constantinople, in Turkey, was the cultural center of Europe and one of the world's most powerful cities.

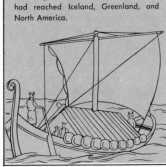

Polynesians were roaming the Pacific and settling on islands there. Some went as far east as Easter Island.

1066

William the Conqueror, duke of Normandy, invaded England and established a new line of kings.

The hardy Northmen, sailing in open boats, had reached Iceland, Greenland, and North America.

The Chinese had invented printing and were using movable earthenware type.

1189

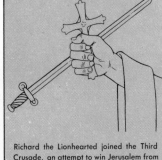

Richard the Lionhearted joined the Third Crusade, an attempt to win Jerusalem from the Mohammedans.

The first universities were being developed in cities in Italy and France.

The Inca Indians had founded a rich empire in Peru. They ruled much of northwestern South America.

1337

Giotto, great Italian painter of the early Renaissance, died. The Renaissance was soon to spread throughout Europe.

In Russia raiding Tartars from Asia had set up the Empire of the Golden Horde.

The Aztecs had founded an empire in central Mexico which was to last until the arrival of the Spaniards.

1453

Constantinople fell to the Turks, and the Eastern, or Byzantine, Empire that had lasted 1,000 years ended.

Printing had just been invented in Europe. Paper had been introduced into Spain by the Moors.

Joan of Arc had helped the French win a victory at Orléans in the Hundred Years' War between England and France.

1492

Columbus made his first trip to the Americas. The American Indians had still not advanced beyond the Stone Age.

Renaissance art had reached its peak in the work of Raphael, Michelangelo, and Leonardo da Vinci.

The Moors had been driven out of Spain by the armies of Ferdinand and Isabella. Spain began playing a large role in European affairs.

1543

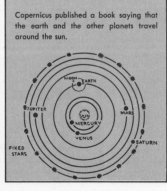

Copernicus published a book saying that the earth and the other planets travel around the sun.

Spaniards had conquered the Aztec and Inca empires and ruled much of the Americas.

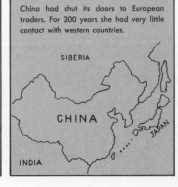

China had shut its doors to European traders. For 300 years she had very little contact with western countries.

1620

The Pilgrims landed at Plymouth and started a colony. They survived the first winter with the help of some friendly Indians.

Shakespeare had just died in England, leaving behind his great plays and poems.

In Italy, Galileo showed people how to gain scientific knowledge by experimenting.

1769

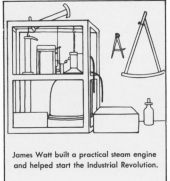

James Watt built a practical steam engine and helped start the Industrial Revolution.

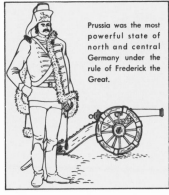

Prussia was the most powerful state of north and central Germany under the rule of Frederick the Great.

Russia was ruled by the empress Catherine the Great. During her reign, Russia gained territory in eastern Europe.

1781

The American colonies gained their freedom by defeating England in the American Revolution.

There was much unrest in France under King Louis XVI, which soon led to the French Revolution.

Captain Cook had explored the east coast of Australia and had claimed the huge island for England.

1837

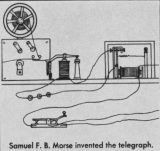

Samuel F. B. Morse invented the telegraph. The age when messages could be sent rapidly from place to place began.

Spanish rule in South America had been ended by the great military leader Simón Bolívar.

SOUTH AMERICA

Napoleon had lost the great empire he had built up, and France was once again ruled by a king.

1863

Abraham Lincoln signed the Emancipation Proclamation, freeing the slaves in the South.

Explorers in Africa were becoming aware of some of the riches there. The scramble for African colonies was soon to begin.

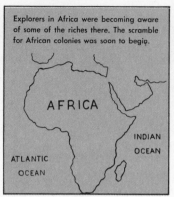

The discovery of gold in southern Australia had brought many people to that new land.

1903

An airplane built by the Wright brothers flew at Kitty Hawk, N. C. It was man's first successful powered flight.

Queen Victoria had just died. Under her rule, the British Empire had become more powerful than ever before.

The German Empire was growing fast, acquiring possessions in Africa and in the Pacific Ocean.

1918

World War I ended after four years of fighting. Many new countries were formed in Europe.

The Russians had overthrown their czar and were working out a communist form of government.

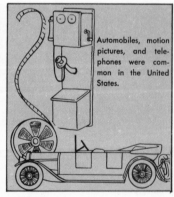

Automobiles, motion pictures, and telephones were common in the United States.

1933

Adolf Hitler became chancellor of Germany and embarked on a series of conquests that led to World War II.

Japan seized Manchuria from China and occupied it. Japan had become one of the world's powerful nations.

Charles Lindbergh had made the first nonstop solo flight across the Atlantic Ocean going from New York to Paris.

1942

The Atomic Age began when scientists successfully achieved the first controlled atomic chain reaction.

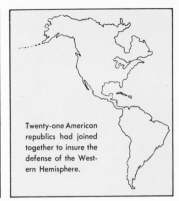

World War II was being waged. Almost all the countries in the world were involved.

Twenty-one American republics had joined together to insure the defense of the Western Hemisphere.

1945

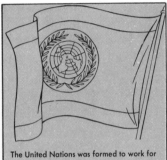

The United Nations was formed to work for peace and for making the lives of people of all lands better in many ways.

World War II ended. Disagreements between the Soviet Union and the U. S., England, and France developed, leading to the "cold war."

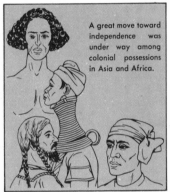

A great move toward independence was under way among colonial possessions in Asia and Africa.

1949

Ten democracies of western Europe joined the United States and Canada to form the North Atlantic Treaty Organization.

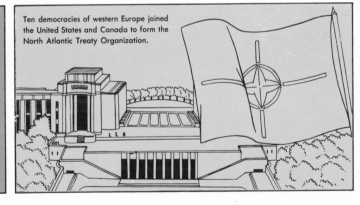

Communism had spread into southeastern Europe, and over China and North Korea.

1958

In January the United States launched its first earth satellite, shortly after the U.S.S.R. had sent up Sputnik I.

In certain remote parts of the world where they are untouched by civilization, people were still living in the Stone Age.

Rock
Collection

HOBBIES In the days when most work was done by hand there was not much time for fun. Even children sometimes worked 15 or 16 hours a day. For grownups eight hours is now the ordinary work day. For boys and girls school lasts only about six hours a day, and there is a long summer vacation. Almost everyone has a great deal of time to spend as he pleases. Much spare time is now spent on hobbies. A hobby is making or doing or learning something just for the fun of it. Any hobby would be work if one had to do it; it is play since it does not have to be done.

Making a collection is the commonest hobby. People collect all sorts and kinds of things. China animals, glass bottles, silver spoons, butterflies, and stamps are a few of them. Stamps are the most popular of all. Some stamp collectors have collections worth many thousands of dollars.

Painting is the hobby of a great many people. Some other popular hobbies are raising flowers, knitting, hiking, mountain climbing, singing, playing a musical instrument, building furniture, sewing, making pottery, studying the stars, doing puzzles, and learning a new language. Hobby shows are held in many places. It is surprising what strange and unusual hobbies one finds out about at these shows.

A hobby sometimes stops being a hobby and becomes a person's work. A man who has been raising flowers as a hobby may start raising them to sell. A woman who likes to sew may start doing it for a living. A child's hobby may become his work when he grows up. Audubon spent much of his spare time as a boy watching birds. As a man he made himself famous by his beautiful pictures of birds. Raymond L. Ditmars had a hobby of collecting snakes as a boy. He grew up to be a world authority on reptiles and became head of the reptile section of a big zoo.

Doctors tell us that being very much interested in something helps our minds stay well. It is good, therefore, for a person to have a hobby. Of course, he may have more than one. When a child goes to a new school, or when a grown person wants a new job, he often has to answer a long list of questions. His answers tell a great deal about what kind of person he is. One of the questions is almost sure to be, "What are your hobbies?" (See AUDUBON.)

Leaf
Collection

HOCKEY In vacant lots and empty streets boys sometimes play shinny. They use crooked sticks and a tin can. Each team tries to knock the tin can through the goal of the other team. When shinny is played on a grass-covered field with carefully made sticks and a leather-covered ball, it is called field hockey.

There are 11 persons on each team in field hockey. A game is made up of two halves not more than 30 minutes long.

Field hockey is played in many schools. Most of the teams are made up of girls. The boys play football or soccer instead.

When men play hockey they usually play it on ice. Ice hockey is now one of the leading sports in the United States and in Canada. There are ice hockey leagues just as there are basketball, baseball, and football leagues.

In ice hockey there are only six men on each team. A disk of rubber called a puck is used instead of a ball. There are three 20-minute periods in a game. If the score is tied at the end of the third period, an extra 10-minute period is played.

Ice hockey is a very fast game. The puck travels nearly 90 miles an hour over the ice. Of course, a good player has to be an excellent skater.

It would seem very strange for a football or a basketball team to play with fewer men than there are on the other team. But one team in a hockey game is often shorthanded for a while. If a player makes a foul, he is put in the penalty box. He must stay there for two, five, or ten minutes. No one takes his place on the ice while he is in the penalty box. A hockey player helps his team by being careful to follow the rules. (See BASEBALL; BASKETBALL; FOOTBALL; SOCCER.)

Face-off

Body Block

Goalie Defending Net

Moving the Puck

New Year's Day	January 1
Lincoln's Birthday	February 12
Valentine's Day	February 14
Washington's Birthday	February 22
St. Patrick's Day	March 17
April Fools' Day	April 1
Palm Sunday	Sunday before Easter
Good Friday	Friday before Easter
Easter	In March or April (movable)
Arbor Day	Movable
May Day	May 1
Mother's Day	Second Sunday in May
Memorial Day	May 30
Flag Day	June 14
Father's Day	Third Sunday in June
Independence Day	July 4
Labor Day	First Monday in September
Yom Kippur	Movable
Columbus Day	October 12
Halloween	October 31
Election Day	First Tuesday after first Monday in November
Veterans' Day	November 11
Thanksgiving	Fourth Thursday in November
Hanukkah (Festival of Lights)	Movable
Christmas	December 25

HOLIDAYS The word "holiday" comes from the words "holy day." Holidays were first religious festivals. Now many holidays have nothing to do with religion. Almost every country has holidays honoring important events or people in its history.

Some holidays are celebrated in many countries. Some are observed in just one. Some are celebrated in only one part of one country. Some are celebrated by he people of only one religion.

Halloween always comes on the same date of the same month. Many other holidays do. But some do not. Some, such as Easter, are movable holidays. Easter is the first Sunday after the first full moon after the beginning of spring. It can be as early as March 22, or as late as April 25.

Every person has his own private holiday when he is given gifts by his family and friends. It is his birthday.

The list beside the picture names 25 of the holidays most widely celebrated in the United States. It also tells when each of these holidays is celebrated.

HOLLY Almost everyone thinks of a sprig of shiny green leaves and red berries when he hears the word "holly," because sprigs of holly are common at Christmas time. Holly is really a kind of tree. It grows about 50 feet tall and is shaped like a pyramid. Its trunk may be two or even three feet in diameter. The bark is smooth.

Before there are berries, there are white flowers on a holly tree. The berries grow from the white flowers.

Holly is an evergreen with shiny, tough leaves.

Holly wood is very white. It is much used for fancy carving and woodwork.

There are about 175 kinds of holly. Some kinds have red, others yellow, and still others black berries. Most of the many kinds of holly grow in South America. In the United States holly is found in the southern states and along the Pacific coast. It is shipped far and wide from these regions for Christmas decorations.

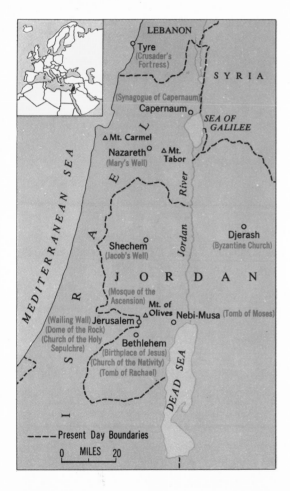

HOLY LAND For centuries and centuries Palestine, at the eastern end of the Mediterranean Sea, was the home of the Jews. Christians call it the Holy Land because it is the land where Jesus lived.

In the days of Jesus, Palestine was a part of the great Roman Empire. A few hundred years later Palestine was conquered by the Arabs. The Arabs were followers of Mohammed. To them the land is holy, too.

During the Middle Ages the Christians of western Europe fought the wars called the Crusades to try to take the Holy Land away from the Mohammedans. They had some success. But in the end all Palestine was once more in Mohammedan hands.

After the first World War Palestine was put under the protection of the British. After the second World War there was a great deal of arguing and even fighting about it. The Jews wished to set up a new nation of their own. The Arabs wished it for themselves. In the end it was divided between the two peoples. The part of the Holy Land that now belongs to the Jews is called Israel. (See CHRISTIANITY; CRUSADES; ISRAEL; JERUSALEM; JESUS; JEWS; MOHAMMED.)

HOMER Two of the world's most famous poems are the *Iliad* and the *Odyssey*. The *Iliad* is the story of the Trojan War. The *Odyssey* is the story of the wanderings of the Greek hero Ulysses after the Trojan War. The poems are so long that each one fills an entire book.

The author of these poems, Greek legends say, was a blind poet named Homer. But no one knows anything about Homer. No one knows when or where he was born. There are pictures and busts of Homer, but they are based only on imagination. Some people think that there never was such a person. Other people think that Homer really lived but that he did not write the poems. They believe that he was a minstrel who went about singing poems that had been made up in earlier times. It is surely true that the Greeks told the stories of Ulysses and the Trojan War long before anyone wrote them down.

Whether there ever was a Homer does not really matter. For we have the poems, and they are two of the greatest poems of their kind ever written. They have lived for more than 2,500 years and are still widely read. (See ACHILLES; LITERATURE; MYTHS AND LEGENDS; TROJAN WAR.)

HOMES "There's no place like home," the song "Home, Sweet Home" tells us. But home for one person may be very different from home for another. For one it may mean a room dug out of a cliff of clay. For another it may mean a house up on stilts near a seashore. For one it may mean a big brick house with many rooms. For another it may mean a tent of skin. It may mean an apartment 20 stories above the street, a grass hut, a stone cottage, an igloo, or even a boat tied up to a river bank. The pictures show how different homes can be.

Homes are different partly because they are made of different materials. A man in a jungle in Africa could not build a snow igloo even if he wanted to. An Eskimo could not have a house made of banana leaves and bamboo.

Houses are different partly because they are built to fit different climates. In a land with cold winters a person wants a snug house that will shut out the cold winter winds and will keep the heat from his fire inside. In a hot, rainy land, one wants a house with a roof that will shed rain easily and with walls that are open enough to let breezes blow through.

A person's home, moreover, must fit his way of living. A nomad would not want a sturdy house built of brick or stone. He has to have a home that he can fold up and carry with him when he moves his herds to new pastures.

The first lasting houses we know about were little one-room round huts built over deep pits in the ground. The low walls were of stone or clay or wood. There were prob-

ably no windows or chimneys. These homes could not have been very pleasant. In winter, living in them must have been a good deal like living inside a stove.

In the thousands of years since these first houses were built, people have learned to build better and better houses. A person who lived in one of the early round houses would marvel if he could come into a modern house. The plumbing, the electric lights, the big windows, the soundproof walls, and the furnace, stove, and refrigerator would seem to him like magic.

One of the pictures shows an apartment house. The idea of building many homes together is not new. Back in ancient Rome there were apartment buildings several stories high. They were made of concrete and wood and were called "islands." But in our apartments we have many comforts Roman apartments did not have.

Many people imagine that the castles of the Middle Ages were wonderful homes. They *were* wonderful compared with the huts that were clustered near their walls. But castles were cold and damp and gloomy. They were poor compared with modern homes.

Modern homes can be built in many styles. Thousands of people earn their living by planning houses that will be convenient, comfortable, and attractive. Many experiments with new materials are constantly going on. Some day people may have houses even better than the houses of today, just as we have houses far ahead of those of long ago. (See ARCHITECTURE; BUILDING MATERIALS.)

Cave Home

Indian Tepee

Modern Apartment House

Modern House

African Hut

Indian Cliff Dwelling

Igloo

Log Cabin

Pioneer Sod Hut

Medieval Castle

Thatched Cottage

Indian Adobe House

Lake Dwelling

Arab Tent

Alpine Chalet

Southern Mansion

Chinese Houseboat

East Indian Grass-roofed House

Half-timber House

Laplander Hut

Roman House

Homing Pigeon with Message Container

HOMING PIGEONS Most birds find their way back to their homes easily. But homing pigeons are especially good at doing so. Because they are good at finding their way home over long distances, people have used them as messengers for many centuries. The Egyptians sent messages by them at least as early as 1200 B.C. Of course, homing pigeons are only able to carry messages home.

The message to be carried is fastened to the pigeon. Usually it is in a small container attached to the bird's leg.

Homing pigeons travel fast. One pigeon carried a message 90 miles in 110 minutes. Another flew 40 miles in 40 minutes.

Although these pigeons are naturally good messengers, they can be trained to be better ones. They can, for instance, be trained to fly faster and to go into their loft the minute they reach it.

Homing pigeons have been especially helpful as message carriers in wartime. Several pigeons became war heroes. At Verdun, in France, for instance, there is a plaque honoring homing pigeon No. 183/140F. In World War I this pigeon carried a message which saved Verdun.

In these days of electronics pigeons are less important as message carriers than they used to be. In 1956 the United States Army decided that it no longer needed any pigeon messengers.

Homing pigeon races are held from time to time. But in many of the races since World War II large numbers of pigeons have failed to reach home. Some pigeon raisers blame TV aerials, hawks, or bad weather. Others blame radar or atom bomb testing. No one can really tell what is to blame, for no one yet knows how pigeons ever find their way home. (See PIGEONS.)

HONG KONG On some small maps of huge China, Hong Kong looks as if it were a part of that country. It is not. But it borders southeastern China, and is not far from southern China's big city, Canton. Hong Kong is a British Crown Colony.

Though Hong Kong is small in size, it is an important bit of the great British Commonwealth. And it has three parts. Two parts have been owned by the British since the middle of the 1800's. They are a small peninsula in Asia's mainland, and the hilly little nearby island of Hong Kong. Every

Hong Kong has a beautiful natural harbor.

day ferryboats carry hundreds of people between those parts. The ferryboat trip is only about a mile long. The third part is some territory next door to the peninsula. In 1898 the British leased it from China for 99 years.

The cities of Victoria and Kowloon both border Hong Kong's great harbor. That safe, roomy harbor is deep enough for the largest ship ever built. Ships big and small from near and far help the vast trade that goes on there. This trade helps thousands of British and hundreds of thousands of Chinese to make a living in Hong Kong. And it has helped to make Hong Kong famous throughout the world.

HOOFED ANIMALS The feet of a tiger and a horse are very different. The toes of a tiger end in sharp claws. A horse's toes end in hoofs. Claws are very helpful to a meat-eating animal. Hoofs are much better than claws for a plant-eating animal that walks about to graze.

There are a great many hoofed animals. Another name for them is "ungulates." This name comes from a Latin word meaning "nail" or "hoof."

All hoofed animals are plant eaters. Many of them chew a cud. They all live on the ground and move about by walking or running. Some of them are very swift. Others are rather slow and clumsy. No hoofed animals are tree-climbers. Many of them can swim, but only a few spend much time in the water.

Some hoofed animals have an even number of toes. The others, of course, have an odd number. The list names some of each:

Odd-toes: Donkey, horse, rhinoceros, tapir, zebra.

Even-toes: Alpaca, antelope, bison, camel, cow, deer, giraffe, goat, hippopotamus, llama, pig, sheep, vicuña, yak, zebu.

It is easy to see from the list that hoofed animals are very important to us. Many of the animals we have tamed are in this group. Most of our meat and all our milk comes from hoofed animals. (See DOMESTICATED ANIMALS; HERBIVOROUS ANIMALS; MAMMALS.)

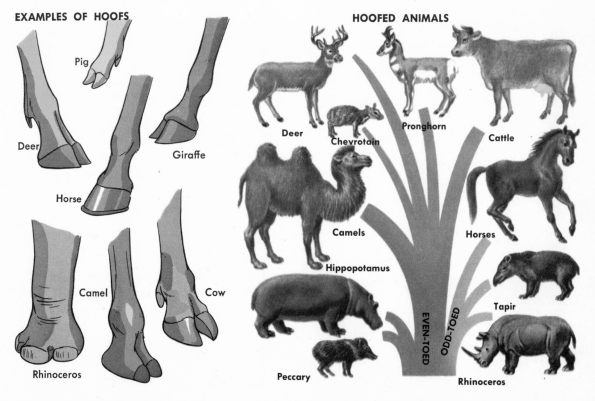

EXAMPLES OF HOOFS — Pig, Deer, Giraffe, Horse, Camel, Cow, Rhinoceros

HOOFED ANIMALS — Deer, Chevrotain, Pronghorn, Cattle, Camels, Hippopotamus, Horses, Tapir, Peccary, Rhinoceros — EVEN-TOED, ODD-TOED

Mesohippus was the size of a collie dog.

HORSES Fifty million years ago some small animals no bigger than foxes ran about in the swampy forests of North America. These little animals had short necks and manes made of a few stiff hairs. Their tails were small. Their teeth were fitted for eating only tender leaves. On each front foot they had four toes. On each hind foot they had three. These small animals were "dawn horses." Small though they were, they were the ancestors of all our horses of today. The scientists' name for the little dawn horse is *Eohippus*.

As millions of years passed, conditions on the earth changed. The dawn horses changed, too. After many, many generations they were larger. They had longer necks, heavier manes and tails, and fewer toes. The middle toe on each foot, moreover, had a heavier nail. It was the beginning of a hoof. They were so different from *Eohippus* that scientists have given them another name—*Mesohippus*.

Horses kept on changing. At last they were much like the horses of today. All the toes disappeared except the middle ones. On these toes there were good hoofs. The

horses ran about on the tips of their toes—on their heavy toenails.

Then a strange thing happened. All the horses in North America disappeared. Perhaps they crossed into Asia, for long ago Asia was joined to North America by a land bridge. At least there were wild horses in Asia and Europe in the days of cave men.

The cave men hunted horses just as they hunted mammoths. They wanted them for food. Perhaps when horses were first tamed they were raised for their meat and their milk. But they soon came to be more valued as beasts of burden.

In ancient times and all through the Middle Ages one of the most important uses of the horse was to help in wars. Ancient Egyptian and Assyrian rulers went to battle in chariots drawn by horses. The knights of the Middle Ages had suits of armor for their horses as well as for themselves.

Many people think that there were wild horses on the plains of North America when Columbus discovered America. They think that the Indians caught and tamed these wild horses. This idea is wrong. The Indians had never seen horses until the Spaniards brought them. The Spaniards would not have won such easy victories over the Indians if it had not been for their horses. Some of the Spanish horses escaped. The wild horses the Indians tamed in later years were descendants of these Spanish horses.

Our horses of today have been pretty much "made to order." For some purposes speed is much more important than strength. For some purposes it was better to have little horses, for other purposes big

Eohippus
(Dawn Horse)

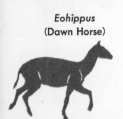

Mesohippus
(In-between Horse)

Protohippus
(Just-before Horse)

ones. Hundreds of years ago, people began changing horses to suit themselves. They developed different kinds of horses to help in different ways. The pictures show some of the kinds of horses we have today.

Some people think that the word "Thoroughbred" means purebred. But the horse we call the Thoroughbred is a special kind of purebred horse. The horses that run in running races are Thoroughbreds. Thoroughbreds are also used as riding horses, polo ponies, and hunting horses.

All Thoroughbreds are part Arabian horse. The Arabs for centuries have been famous for their horses. Thoroughbreds began with the mating of English mares and Arab stallions. There are still many purebred Arabian horses.

Morgan horses are good harness horses. They are good riding horses, too. All Morgan horses came from a colt that an American boy named Henry Morgan raised.

The American Saddle Horse is another horse that was developed in America. This breed gives us the gaited horses that are so important in horse shows.

The Percheron is a very heavy horse. It is one of the several kinds of draft horses. No one would enter a Percheron in a race with a Thoroughbred. But the heavy draft horses can pull very heavy loads.

Palomino horses are popular as riding horses now. They can be told by their light

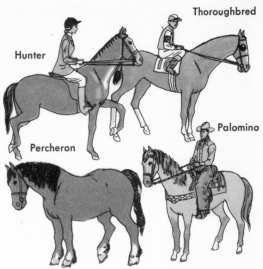

Hunter
Thoroughbred
Percheron
Palomino

tan or cream coloring and white manes. Like the Thoroughbreds, they have a great deal of Arab in them.

For children small horses are needed. Small horses are best for certain kinds of work, too. Ponies of different kinds were therefore developed. The Shetlands are the most famous. They originally came from the Shetland Islands.

In 1920 there were more than 25 million horses in the United States. In 1957 there were less than 4 million. Cars, trucks, and tractors are taking the place of horses. But horses will always be raised, for machines can never wholly take their place. (See CHARIOT; DOMESTICATED ANIMALS; HOOFED ANIMALS; INDIANS; PONY EXPRESS; RODEO.)

Modern Horse

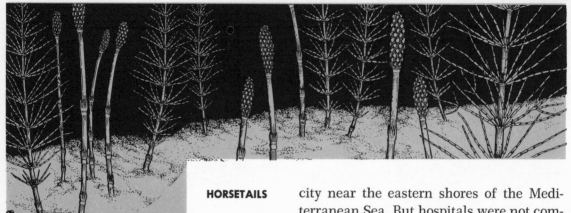

HORSETAILS

HORSETAILS Small plants called horse-tails are often found on cinder slopes along railroad tracks, where almost no other plants will grow. They are found, too, in barren, sandy regions and along the damp edges of swamps.

These plants are sometimes called "joint grass" because their stems are jointed. The main stem of a horsetail is underground. The stems aboveground are about as big around as soda straws and are hollow except at the joints. Horsetails have no leaves. Each joint on the stem has a circle of "teeth" which are really relics of leaves horsetails of long ago had. The green stems now do the food-making which leaves do for most other green plants.

Horsetails are sometimes called "scour-ing rushes." Their stems are so gritty that they can be used to scour pots and pans.

The horsetails are cousins of the ferns and the club mosses. Like their cousins, they have spores, not seeds. Since horse-tails are not seed plants, they do not have flowers. Their spores are formed in cones.

Some of the horsetails of long ago were very large. In the swampy forests of the Coal Age there were tree horsetails. But in time flowering plants crowded them out. (See CLUB MOSSES; FERNS.)

HOSPITALS Building a place where sick people can be cared for is not a new idea. A hospital was built as long ago as A.D. 369. It was founded by a bishop in Caesarea, a city near the eastern shores of the Medi-terranean Sea. But hospitals were not com-mon for a very long time. In Europe during the Middle Ages monks helped care for the sick. Many of the early monasteries were partly hospitals.

In the hospitals of today sick people are looked after by both doctors and nurses. Doctors have everything they need for ex-amining and treating their patients. They have wonderful operating rooms. There are always doctors at hand to look after emer-gency cases. As a rule anyone badly hurt in an accident is rushed to a hospital. Hos-pitals serve another important purpose, too. Doctors study diseases there and work out better ways of treating them.

Some hospitals of today are general hos-pitals. They take in cases of all kinds. Others are special hospitals. They may be for children only, for people with conta-gious diseases, for people who are crippled, for mentally sick patients, or for women who are having babies.

In some hospitals the patients pay for their care. In others they do not. In many

Hospital care is constantly improving.

hospitals the government or some charity pays the expenses.

Not many years ago hospitals were rather cheerless places. They had a disagreeable hospital smell, too, that came from the chemicals used in killing germs. Now many hospital rooms are gay and cheerful. And the hospital smell is gone. Doctors have found out that most patients get well faster if their surroundings are pleasant.

HOTELS When people began making long journeys, they needed places to stop for the night. Inns were built.

The first inns we know about were in lands at the eastern end of the Mediterranean Sea. The rooms were built around a court where horses and donkeys and camels could be kept.

The skyscraper hotel below shows what inns have grown into today. A hotel like the one in the picture may have room for hundreds of people. It has large dining rooms and rooms where big meetings can be held. The biggest hotel in the world is the Conrad Hilton Hotel in Chicago. In it there are 3,000 rooms. Of course, not all modern hotels are big. There are still many rather small inns.

Big hotels can be divided into three kinds. There are resort hotels, where people go for a vacation. They are mostly near the seashore or lake shore or in the mountains.

There are commercial hotels, usually in the heart of a city. Always in such a hotel there are many people who have come to the city on business. The third kind of hotel is a residence hotel. People may make their homes in residence hotels for weeks or months or even years.

Big hotels have worked out many ways of making their guests comfortable. Many rooms are air-conditioned. In many there are television sets. In most rooms there are telephones. Ice water is almost always at hand. Clothes can be cleaned and pressed in a very short time. Meals can be served in the rooms. In many big hotels there are exhibit rooms, ballrooms, flower shops, gift shops, barber shops, beauty shops, drugstores, and dress shops.

A new kind of hotel has sprung up in recent years—a kind of hotel for people who are traveling by car. This kind of a hotel is called a motel. "Motel" is short for "motoring hotel." A person in a car can drive right up to the door of his room. In some motels the service is as good as in big hotels. Some motels are in beautiful settings.

Hotels are a big business. There are more than 50,000 hotels and motels in the United States alone. There are several big chains of hotels. It is possible to visit many cities in the United States and even some in other countries, and still always stay in hotels of the same chain.

Old English Inn

Motel

Modern Hotel

Poás Crater
Costa Rica

Roman Bath
England

Yellowstone
United States

HOT SPRINGS Springs where cold water comes bubbling out of the ground are common. Springs of hot water are not nearly as common. But there are hot springs in a number of different places.

The water in hot springs gets its heat from very hot rock not far below the surface of the ground. A hole dug down deep enough anywhere on the earth would come to hot rock. Most of the places where the hot rock is rather close to the top of the ground are near volcanoes, either dead ones or ones that are still active.

For a hot spring there must be a tube, or channel, in which water can gather. The tube must reach upward from the hot rock to the surface of the ground. As cold water flows into the tube it sinks to the bottom. The moving of cold water to the bottom pushes the hot water out of the top.

Many hot springs have "craters" around them. These craters are built of minerals dissolved in the hot water. When the water comes out of the spring it gets cool. Then it cannot hold as many minerals as it held when it was hot. Some of the water, moreover, evaporates. As it does, it leaves its minerals behind. Besides, in the water there are tiny plants called algae. They help make the water drop its minerals.

The "craters" around hot springs often have beautiful colors in them. The water itself may be colored, too. The colors come from the algae.

Some algae can live in water that is almost hot enough to boil. For other algae the water must be cooler. The colors that are found most in the pools around hot springs are creamy white, salmon pink, orange, brown, yellow, and green.

Some hot springs do not spill over. The water evaporates as fast as it is pushed up from below. If the water is colored by algae, these springs are called "paint pots."

Yellowstone National Park has hundreds of hot springs. Hot Springs, Arkansas, was named for nearby hot springs. Part of the name of Iceland's capital, Reykjavík (RAY kya veek), means "smoking." The "smoke" is steam from hot springs there.

The people of Iceland have put their hot springs to good use. They pipe water from them to heat their houses. In other parts of the world there are health resorts near hot springs. People often come long distances to bathe in the water. The English city of Bath has been famous for its hot-spring baths since the days of ancient Rome. (See ALGAE; GEYSERS; NATIONAL PARKS; VOLCANOES.)

HOUSEBOATS Some people live their whole lives on boats without ever seeing much of the world. They live on houseboats. Houseboats usually are not built so they can travel by themselves. When a family that lives on a houseboat wants to move, they usually have to have their boat towed to another place.

Houseboats are very common in China. The banks of rivers near towns and cities are often lined with them. They are common on the rivers in the hot lands of South America, too. On some rivers they are often so close together that a person can walk a long way by stepping from boat to boat. In the United States there are many houseboats in Florida. There are some on many rivers in other states. There are even a few on the Chicago River in the heart of the big city of Chicago.

People live on houseboats for different reasons. In China a family may live on a houseboat because they do not have any land for a house. In South America a family may live on a houseboat because it is hard to cut down enough trees to clear a space for a house. In the United States people live in houseboats partly because they like the idea of being able to move whenever they want to.

There are many ways in which living on a houseboat is fun. But there are some things against it. A houseboat cannot be very large because then it would be too clumsy to be moved about easily. The people who live on houseboats usually have very crowded quarters. Getting good water is another problem. Even though there is water all around the boat, the water a houseboat is floating on is never safe to drink. Getting rid of rubbish is a problem, too. There is no back yard for a bonfire, and there is no garbage collector. Often, moreover, the dampness is a nuisance. People who live on houseboats cannot have many of the conveniences people in ordinary houses have. It is easy to see why most people prefer a house to a houseboat.

Oriental Sampan

Chinese Junk

Houseboat

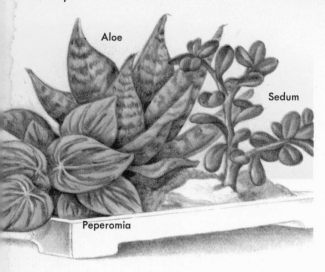

Aloe

Sedum

Peperomia

HOUSE PLANTS People who like flowers can have them the year round. They can have them even in the middle of winter. For there are many plants that will bloom indoors. Some plants are pretty just because of their leaves, not their flowers. Many of these, too, will grow very well indoors. All the plants that can be kept indoors are called house plants.

Many house plants are started in greenhouses. They are sold when they are old enough to be pretty. At Christmas time and Easter time flower shops sell huge numbers of potted plants.

After these plants come into our houses they may live for a long time. Or they may die very soon. How long they live depends mostly on how well they are taken care of. Not all house plants should be treated the same way. Some need to be in bright sunlight; others cannot stand it. Some need water every day; others should not be watered as often. Some need more warmth than others. Some cannot stand drafts. Some should have extra plant food once in a while. Often a plant that comes from a flower shop has a card with it that tells how to take care of the plant.

Not all house plants come from flower shops. It is fun to raise one's own plants. If a person has an African violet or a begonia, he can raise new plants from the leaves of the plant he has. Foliage plants, philodendron, and sansevieria can be raised from slips. A slip is a small branch of a plant.

Some house plants can be raised from bulbs. The bulbs may not need any soil at all. Paper-white narcissus bulbs, for example, will grow and bloom if they are planted in pebbles and water.

A very pretty vine can be raised from a common sweet potato. It needs only to be stood up in a jar of water. Beautiful feathery little plants will grow from the top halves of carrots.

Some house plants can even be raised indoors from seeds. Morning-glory and nasturtium are two that can be. They will bloom indoors if they have just the right amounts of water and warmth and sunshine, and if their pots are the right size Grapefruit seeds will not grow into grapefruit trees indoors, but they will grow into pretty plants with shiny leaves.

Whole little gardens can be raised in glass "greenhouses" indoors. The greenhouse may be a big glass bottle or a fish bowl with a glass cover or a container bought at a flower shop. Little plants such as mosses and tiny ferns can be gathered outdoors for it. A garden of this kind is called a terrarium. Many people make terrariums a hobby. (See BULBS; GREENHOUSE; HOBBIES.)

African Violet

C

THE GOLDEN BOOK ENCYCLOPEDIA

CONTAINS THE FOLLOWING VOLUMES

CONTRIBUTING ARTISTS

Dot and Sy Barlowe • Cornelius De Witt • E. Joseph Dreany • Bruno Frost
James Gordon Irving • Beth and Joe Krush • Harry Lazarus • Andre LeBlanc
H. Charles McBarron • Denny McMains • Harry McNaught
Ray Perlman • John Polgreen • Evelyn Urbanowich

Pauline Batchelder Adams • George Avison • Barry Bart • Ernie Barth • Charles Bellow
Eric Bender • Juanita Bennett • Merrit Berger • Robert D. Bezucha • William Bolin
Thelma Bowie • Matilda Breuer • S. Syd Brown • Peter Buchard • Louise Fulton Bush
Jim Caraway • Nino Carbe • Sam Citron • Gordon Clifton • Mel Crawford • Robert Doremus
Harry Daugherty • Rachel Taft Dixon • Olive Earle • Sydney F. Fletcher • F. Beaumont Fox
Rudolf Freund • Tibor Gergely • Douglas Gorsline • Hamilton Greene • Gerald Gregg
Marjorie Hartwell • Hans H. Helweg • Janice Holland • W. Ben Hunt
Arch and Miriam Hurford • Harper Johnson • Norman Jonsson • Matthew Kalmenoff
Janet Robson Kennedy • Paul Kinnear • Olga Kucera • Walter Kumme • John Leone
Kenneth E. Lowman • John Alan Maxwell • Jean McCammack • Shane Miller • Stina Nagel
Elizabeth Newhall • Gregory Orloff • Raymond Pease • Alice and Martin Provensen
Jerry Robinson • Feodor Rojankovsky • Roki • Mary Royt • Arnold W. Ryan
Arthur Sanford • Sam Savitts • William Sayles • Al Schmidt • Edwin Schmidt
Frederick E. Seyfarth • Robert Sherman • George Solonewitsch • Lionel Stern
Norton Stewart • Valerie Swenson • Gustaf Tenggren • William Thompson • Felix Traugott
Eileen Fox Vaughn • Herschel Wartik • Robert Weisman • Garth Williams

MAPS BY

Vincent Kotschar   Jean Paul Tremblay
Carol Vinall   Frederic Lorenzen
Rudolf von Siegl   Francis Barkoczy

COVER ARTISTS

Ned Seidler • Ken Davies • Don Moss